*The Master Musicians Series*

# BRAHMS

SERIES EDITED BY

SIR JACK WESTRUP,
M.A., Hon. D.Mus.(Oxon.), F.R.C.O.

Brahms listening to the Joachim Quartet at the house of his friends, the Wittgensteins, during the winter of 1895–6. The artist is Paul Wittgenstein, brother of the owner of the house. When Paul died the sketch passed to his nephew, the late Paul Wittgenstein (the pianist), and a photograph of it is in the possession of Miss Margaret Deneke. It is by the courtesy of Miss Deneke and Mr. Wittgenstein that it is reproduced here.

THE MASTER MUSICIANS SERIES

# BRAHMS

*by*

# PETER LATHAM

*With eight pages of plates
and music examples in the text*

LONDON
J. M. DENT AND SONS LTD

FARRAR, STRAUS AND GIROUX, INC.
NEW YORK

Made in Great Britain
at the
Aldine Press · Letchworth · Herts
for
J. M. DENT & SONS LTD
Aldine House · Bedford Street · London
First published 1948
Last reprinted 1970

ISBN: 0 460 03104 X

# PREFACE

THE first book on Brahms in the 'Master Musicians' series was written by Lawrence Erb, and appeared in 1905. It went through two reprints, and then, in 1934, came a revised edition with a prefatory note wherein the editor of the series pays a tribute to the careful accuracy of Mr. Erb's work. With that tribute I should like to associate myself. But since 1905 two things have happened against which no author could guard himself: first, our view of the composer and his music has been amplified and sometimes modified as new sources of information became available; secondly, Brahms himself has receded in historical perspective. Mr. Erb wrote only eight years after the death of his subject. Now the eight has become fifty-one—fifty-one of the most eventful years through which the art of music has ever passed. Inevitably the point of view has changed, and the 'Master Musicians' series needs a new volume that reflects that change. This, I imagine, is why the editor has asked me to write one.

I have not, however, interpreted my instructions as a demand for novelty at all costs. Indeed the well-informed reader will find in my pages little that is really new and nothing, I think, that is sensational. But I have tried to see straight—and with the eyes of 1948. I shall be told, of course, that no one can really see straight, no one can avoid having a point of view, even prejudices, that are his own and unique. That is quite true, and it reminds me that I have a confession to make. In reading and thinking about Brahms (the man, not the music) I have developed, rather to my own surprise, a genuine affection for my queer crotchety subject. I am sure it has influenced my judgment, but I cannot be persuaded to regret it.

Every one knows that writing a book is a good way to make enemies. I have also found it a good way to make friends. But for *Brahms* I might never have been led to Gunfield, and missed those pleasant Oxford afternoons when Miss Margaret Deneke put her memories of Brahms's friends at my disposal and showed me her treasures. These include the pencil drawing at the beginning of this volume. It is copied from a work by the

# Preface

late Mr. Paul Wittgenstein (senior), and shows Brahms listening to Mühlfeld and the Joachim Quartet giving the first performance of the clarinet Quintet. Before lending it to me Miss Deneke went to the trouble of communicating with Mr. Paul Wittgenstein (the pianist), so that it is now reproduced with his consent as well as hers. She also put me directly in touch with Mr. Wittgenstein himself, and to him I owe a long and most interesting letter full of Brahms anecdotes that have been preserved in the Wittgenstein family. Several of these anecdotes will be found (with appropriate acknowledgments) scattered through the pages of this book.

It is to Miss Deneke again that I owe my introductions to Mrs. Derenburg (Ilona Eibenschütz) and Mrs. Gombrich, both of whom were kind enough to tell me their recollections of Brahms in Vienna. The photograph of Brahms among his friends (facing p. 135) is reproduced by kind permission of Mrs. Gombrich, to whom it belongs. It was at Gunfield too that I met once more my old friend and teacher, Dr. Ernest Walker, who unlocked his wisdom and knowledge for my benefit, and showed me the Brahms autograph manuscripts in his possession. To Miss Deneke and all these friends of hers I am most heartily obliged.

My thanks are also due to Mr. B. W. Fagan and Mr. S. H. Lovett, who have helped me with books not easy to obtain in these difficult times, and to Miss Rose Stanfield and Mr. Ernest Read, who have lent me music. It was from Mr. Read that I got the superb edition of Brahms's complete works issued under the auspices of the Vienna Philharmonic Society. Without that I could never have completed the Catalogue of Works in Appendix B. I must also acknowledge gratefully the kindness and careful patience of Mr. Godfrey Sampson in the tiresome business of going through my proofs, and thank him for allowing me to reproduce 'Brahms and the Beggar' (facing p. 69). Finally there is my wife. I do not suppose she has the least idea of how much I owe to her advice and encouragement at every stage of the undertaking.

HAMPSTEAD, *June 1948.*                                    P. L.

# PREFACE TO 1962 EDITION

I HAVE taken the opportunity to make a few corrections and alterations of detail for the 1962 reprint, but essentially the book remains as it was when first published in 1948.

P. L.

HAMPSTEAD, *1962*.


# PREFACE TO 1966 EDITION

I HAVE been asked to revise this book with a view to its proposed publication in America, making such alterations as are necessary to bring it completely up to date.

The task presents certain difficulties. I cannot pretend that a book written in 1948 was really written in 1966, nor would the editor wish me to do so. My ideas about Brahms have not changed substantially during the last eighteen years, and my book stands in the main as it stood before.

But one or two new facts have come to light and I have caught myself out in some mistakes and misrepresentations. These I have endeavoured to correct.

It does not amount to very much, yet I think I can say that the volume thus revised contains no voluntary misstatement and is as up to date as I can make it. But it makes no bones about its age.

P. L.

*1966.*

# CONTENTS

## PART I

# ILLUSTRATIONS

TO

ANGELA

# PART I

## CHAPTER I

### THE YOUNG EAGLE

#### § 1. Boyhood (1833–53)

ONE day in Vienna a young girl of eighteen, the daughter of one of his friends, presented Brahms with a thorny spray of dog-rose. He accepted it with a smile and asked, 'Is this an emblem of my prickly nature?'[1] He was perfectly aware that he was feared throughout the city for the uncertainty of his temper and the sharpness of his tongue and derived some grim amusement from the knowledge. He would have thoroughly appreciated the new point that has been given to his little joke by modern etymologists who tell us that the very name 'Brahms' has prickly associations, since it is derived from the same root, 'Bram,' as our English word 'bramble.' To round off the story neatly, 'Bram' should mean 'bramble' in German too. Unfortunately it doesn't. In German 'Bram' is the Plantagenet flower, the *planta genista* or sweet-flowering broom that grows in the lowland country round the mouth of the Elbe.[2]

The family came from lower Saxony. Peter Brahms, the earliest ancester of the composer who has been traced, was a wheelwright,

[1] I have this story from Mr. Paul Wittgenstein.

[2] One still occasionally hears it asserted that 'Brahms' is derived from 'Abrams,' and that Brahms was a Jew. The legend probably has its origin in a quip attributed to Max Bruch. I cannot see that it matters whether he was Jew or gentile, but in the interests of truth I may mention that I have found no reputable authority who supports either the composer's Jewish origin or the 'Abrams' derivation of the name.

and in the middle of the eighteenth century he migrated from the neighbourhood of Hanover to Brunsbüttel, near the Elbe. His second son, Johannes, kept an inn at Heide, in Holstein, and had in his turn two sons. Of these the elder became a dealer in antiques and founded a family that continued to survive in the lower Elbe district, the so-called Ditmarsch country, at any rate till recently. But Johann Jakob (1806–72), the younger son of Johannes, showed quite early in life a passion for music that withstood all his father's efforts at discouragement. He learnt to play several instruments, specializing on the double bass; and to escape the parental opposition he twice ran away from home. In the end his father was compelled to accept the inevitable, and Jakob went off on foot, his double bass on his back, to seek his fortune in the neighbouring city of Hamburg.

Since he had no money and not a particle of influence, since moreover his abilities were no more than ordinary and he remained to the end a mediocre performer, his progress in his chosen profession was slow, and the hardships he had to endure were severe and prolonged. But he faced life with an altogether admirable tenacity and a steady courage, and step by step fought his obscure way forward. His first appointment was in the band of the Hamburg militia, where he is said to have played the horn. But he never abandoned the double bass, and after several years of grinding poverty he managed to get himself enrolled as a regular member of the band of six performers that used to play at the fashionable Alster Pavilion. Later still he got a place as double-bass player in the theatre band. These engagements secured him a living, but only on the barest subsistence level.

Jakob's ambitions were never lofty. He was aware of his limitations and aspired to nothing beyond the career of an ordinary orchestral player. But he never seems to have doubted his ability to make good, and in 1830 he took a sufficiently rosy view of his prospects to embark on matrimony. His bride, Johanna Nissen, whom he married on 9th June, had kept a small haberdashery shop and was an excellent needlewoman. She was short and plain, she limped, and her health was delicate. Worse still, she was seventeen years older than her husband. But there were compensating advantages. Johanna came of a family that could trace its ancestry right back to the fourteenth century, and alliance with her meant a perceptible rise in the social scale for Jakob Brahms. Moreover, she was a sensible, level-headed woman, careful in money matters, who exercised a restraining influence over the optimistic Jakob when, as happened from time to time, he felt tempted to invest his money in a lottery. Sensitive, kindly, affectionate, she made a good home for her husband in spite of their poverty; and when her children arrived she loved them and was loved in return. In the end, it is true, the marriage came to grief. But that was only when Johanna's life was drawing to its close, and by that time her son Johannes was already out in the world. During his boyhood, though life was hard and money scarce, he knew the joys of a happy home and a mother who worshipped him; and he repaid her love with a devotion that never wearied and found its supreme expression in the soprano solo of his Requiem.

He was born on 7th May 1833, in the Brahms home, a first-floor apartment of three small rooms in No. 24 Specksgang, in the Gangeviertel.[1] Light was scarce, for the houses were high and the lanes narrow in this dockside district of Hamburg, a desperately poor and not even respectable quarter known to the sailors as 'Adulterers' Walk.' The fact that honest Jakob and his wife were compelled to live there affords most convincing evidence of their straitened circumstances. Johannes was not the only child. An elder sister, Elise, had been born in 1831, and a younger brother, Friedrich, followed in 1835.

The childhood of Johannes was dominated by two passions, both of which remained with him through life. One was music,

[1] The Gangeviertel has long disappeared, but the house in which Brahms was born stood till it was demolished in the course of the devastating air-raids on Hamburg made during the war of 1939–45.

the other tin soldiers. At the age of twenty-eight he had still not parted with his own little army, which he proudly paraded for the benefit of his friend, Albert Dietrich; and much later the elderly, bearded master could never resist the temptation of arraying the battalions belonging to the children of his landlady, Frau Truxa. As for music, it was fortunate he liked it since it had been decided from his birth that he was to be a musician. Jakob did not set his hopes of his son too high. If 'Hannes' could become an efficient orchestral player, that was all he expected. When he was six his father decided to teach him his notes and with this in view sat down at the piano—only to find the boy, with his back to the instrument, naming each note as soon as it was struck. This was unexpectedly satisfactory. But Jakob was not so pleased when 'Hannes' declared that what he wanted to learn was not an orchestral intrument, but the piano. However, he was not a domineering parent. When his son persisted in his determination he let him have his way, though not without misgivings, and in 1840 Johannes was sent to Otto Cossel to be taught the piano.

Cossel was one of those fine, single-hearted musicians who care more for their art than for their career. His teaching was imaginative as well as conscientious, and he inspired Brahms with lasting love and gratitude. Long after Cossel's death the master paid his tribute when he said that his memory was one of the worthiest and most sacred of his life. The teacher soon recognized the phenomenal talent of his pupil, accepted the heavy responsibility that this imposed upon him, and finally crowned his work by a notable act of self-abnegation. It happened in this way. A travelling agent passing through Hamburg suggested to Jakob that there was money to be made if Johannes would tour America as an infant prodigy. Much attracted by this proposition Jakob consulted Cossel. Fortunately for Johannes Cossel was as wise as he was honest. Realizing the immense harm that the proposed tour would do to his still unformed pupil he opposed the project tooth and nail; and when his arguments fell on deaf ears he did

BRAHMS IN YOUTH
*From Richard Specht, 'Johannes Brahms'*

not hesitate to appeal to his own teacher, the celebrated Eduard Marxsen, universally recognized as the best music-teacher in Hamburg. The self-abnegation consisted in this: Marxsen could not very well intervene unless he himself undertook Johannes' training. Cossel made the sacrifice, relinquished his most brilliant pupil in that pupil's own interests, and exerted himself to the utmost to induce Marxsen to accept him. Marxsen was reluctant, but in the end allowed himself to be persuaded. His influence finally disposed of the American scheme, and Johannes remained in Hamburg under his new teacher.

Here again he was fortunate. Marxsen's teaching was based on a profound study of Bach, a composer whose works were at that time only beginning to win general appreciation, and of Beethoven, whose achievement in the realm of form Marxsen understood far better than most of his contemporaries. His discipline was strict, his manner sometimes harsh. But, like Cossel, he realized that he had genius to deal with and set himself to prune and train with a careful hand. At first his efforts were directed, not without success, towards making his pupil into a virtuoso pianist. Composition was discouraged. But Johannes' enthusiasm was not to be denied, and it soon became impossible to ignore his astonishing creative gift. Here too guidance must be given. The boy's romantic dreams were treated with tenderness in spite of the misgivings they aroused in the somewhat pedantic mind of the teacher, and his instinct for form was welcomed and developed. It was Marxsen who laid the sure foundations of that superb technique which Brahms wielded in his maturity; and he did it without accepting payment. Johannes' confidence in his teacher never wavered. Long after he had entered on his career as a composer he would submit his works to Marxsen for criticism before publication. Even the Requiem did not appear till it had received the hall-mark of the old man's approval. Before he died Marxsen received a tribute that he must have regarded as ample recompense for all his labours: the dedication of the B♮ major piano Concerto.

Concerning the other elements in Brahms's education we have less information. But his parents did all that could be expected, and more. He attended two schools successively, and the second at any rate was a high-grade establishment where, besides the 'three R's,' he obtained some knowledge of French and English. The superstructure of a gentleman's education as regards history, literature and so on he was to acquire in later life by assiduous reading; but sound foundations were laid at school, and he was well educated by the standards of his time and station. The trouble was that economic necessity compelled him to leave school early and contribute his share to the family income. Already in his twelfth year he was giving wretchedly paid music lessons. When he was thirteen he undertook an even more uncongenial task: playing the cheapest of cheap music for the entertainment of the sailors at various taverns in the dock area. For several years Johannes did a great deal of this kind of thing, for which he was paid little but given as much drink as he wanted; and it says much for his strength of character that he did not acquire the habit of intemperance. But the thick reek of beer and tobacco, the noise, the coarse talk revolted the soul of the sensitive child as he sat at the piano, his fingers mechanically grinding out dances, his eyes on the music-stand in front of him, where he had placed, not a sheet of music (he always played by heart), but a volume of poetry by Eichendorff or Heine in whose company he strove to forget his surroundings. There were, however, distractions, some of them of the most revolting kind; for the ladies of the town who frequented these *Lokale* to ply their trade were not always above making use of the boy-pianist to kindle the ardour of their sea-faring admirers.

The subject is unpleasant, but it cannot be disregarded altogether, since Johannes performed his hateful duties for some years, and they made an indelible mark on his character; nor were all the changing events of his career sufficient to erase the nightmare from his memory. There was an occasion in Vienna, late in his life, when, after drinking champagne at a party, he launched unexpectedly into a tirade against the whole tribe of women, growing more and more excited, using increasingly coarse language, till at last he let fall an unprintable word. There had been nothing to provoke the outburst which broke up the gathering in confusion and dismay. Walking home with Max Friedländer Brahms broke a long silence by asking: 'Was it very bad?' 'Yes,' replied Friedländer. The unhappy composer, still labouring under stress of emotion, sought to justify himself. He told Friedländer of his boyhood and the horrors of the Hamburg *Lokale*. 'That,' he cried passionately, 'was my first impression of the love of women. And you expect me to honour them as you do!' It is pleasant to record that after an interval he made an *amende* to his hostess and was forgiven.[1] Like others among his Viennese friends she had much to forgive. But she understood that deep down in his mind there were hidden places, subterranean fires he could not always control.

Unremitting work and the incessant burden of poverty began in time to affect even the sturdy constitution of young Johannes; and he might have broken down altogether but for the kindness of a friend of his father, a patron of the Alster Pavilion, who invited him in the spring of 1847 for a protracted stay in the country. Here at Winsen, in the house of Herr and Frau Giesemann and their daughter Lischen, he got the care and comfort he needed. Here too this child of the Hamburg slums learned for the first time the beauty of garden and meadow, of wood and stream, and loved them as his hero Beethoven had loved them sixty years before at Bonn. He was short-sighted, but not too short-sighted to join in games with the children of the neighbourhood or make expeditions with Lischen; and in these healthy surroundings he recovered his strength. When he came back to Hamburg he was fit and ready to resume both his studies and his drudgery, and his return to Winsen for a shorter visit the following year was prompted not by precarious health, but by friendship alone.

His first public appearance was in 1843, when he played a study

[1] This story comes from Schauffler's *The Unknown Brahms*.

by Herz at a charity concert. But it is not till 1847 that we hear of another concert, not till 1848 of a composition by Brahms himself.[1] On 14th April 1849, however, he gave a concert of his own at which he played, besides Beethoven's 'Waldstein' Sonata, a Fantasia he had written 'on a favourite Waltz.' Strictly speaking these works (which have long vanished) were not the first products of his pen to reach the public, for he seems to have earned something by arranging light music for more than one publisher. But these valueless trifles did not appear under his own name. The real fruits of his studies with Marxsen we know to have been numerous, for he papered the walls of his room with them. But one and all were consigned eventually to the flames. Even the small parcel of compositions that he sent to Schumann when that composer visited Hamburg in 1850 was no exception, for Schumann was too busy to look at it and returned it unopened.

Perhaps it was as well. Schumann had his part to play in the story of Johannes Brahms, but his cue was not yet. For the moment, as Marxsen knew, the vital thing was to get the young man's technical armour firmly riveted from top to toe, and that could best be accomplished in obscure seclusion at Hamburg. What was likely to happen afterwards no one, not even Johannes himself, had any idea. No one, that is, except Marxsen, and he wisely kept his own counsel. Only once did he betray his inmost thoughts when, on Mendelssohn's death in 1847, he said to some friends: 'A master of the art has gone; a greater arises in Brahms.' It would not be long now before his hopes would be put to the test, for Johannes' powers were growing prodigiously. In 1851 he composed the Scherzo in E♭ minor for piano, subsequently published as Op. 4, and this was followed in 1852 by the F♯ minor Sonata, Op. 2. The C major Sonata, Op. 1, was probably begun in 1852, but the bulk of it was written early in 1853. With these pieces before him even Marxsen must have felt content. His task was nearly done.

[1] The evidence regarding this composition is doubtful.

## §2. 'NEW PATHS' (1853)

In 1815 a new and richly coloured personality began to brighten the grey life of the young student. Eduard Reményi was a violinist of mixed Jewish and Hungarian blood. Born in 1830, he got involved as a youth in the revolutionary unrest that disturbed Europe in 1848–9 and arrived in Hamburg as a political refugee. After a stay of some length he passed on to America in 1851. But he was back in 1852 in time to make his brief but picturesque contribution to the life-story of Brahms.

Reményi specialized in the *Zigeuner* (gypsy) style, whose free rhythms and elaborate decorations he would introduce even into his renderings of the classical German masters. But for all his eccentricity he must have been a fiddler of merit to impress Johannes as he did. It was probably in 1850 that they first met; and a friendship arose which eventually bore fruit in a plan to make a small concert tour together during the spring of 1853. The original project was confined to a few towns in the vicinity of Hamburg, and perhaps that is why there is no record of a protest from Marxsen. On 19th April they started off, a curiously assorted couple, with light hearts and light purses, travelling mostly on foot. The first concert was at Winsen, where they were sure of a welcome from Johannes' many friends. Then came Celle, where they had to make do with a piano that was a semitone below pitch, and Brahms astonished Reményi and the audience by transposing Beethoven's C minor violin Sonata into C♯ minor at sight. To Johannes himself, who could play anything in any key, the feat seemed nothing out of the ordinary.

At Hanover Reményi took Brahms to call on Joachim. Though only two years older than Johannes, Joseph Joachim was already reckoned among the greatest violinists of his day. Above and beyond the virtuosity that wins the applause of the vulgar he possessed gifts of insight and understanding that placed him among the very few who could be trusted with such supreme music as Bach's Chaconne or Beethoven's Concerto. His extraordinary

9

ability had early won for him the admiration and friendship of Mendelssohn and subsequently he had become attached to Liszt and his 'neo-German' school. But with the passing of time he grew less sure of his sympathy with Liszt and his aims. Desiring to consider his position in detachment he had left the Liszt head-quarters at Weimar and accepted the position of *Konzertmeister* (leading violinist) to the King of Hanover. He and Reményi had been at school together, and Reményi relied on this link to secure the powerful support of his fellow-countryman. Many years afterwards, at the unveiling of the Brahms memorial at Meiningen in 1899, Joachim gave an account of the interview. He soon saw through Reményi, 'the self-satisfied, fantastic virtuoso.' But his companion, with his short, sturdy figure, his blond hair, smooth cheeks and astonishingly blue eyes, interested him greatly, though he remained silent in the background throughout the conversation. At length Joachim tackled him directly and, finding that he was a composer, asked him to play some of his works. At the piano Brahms's shyness forsook him. He played some sonata movements and the song *Liebestreu*, holding his hearer spellbound with the power of his music, the range of his imagination and the beauty of his playing. Joachim foresaw that the ill-assorted pair would not long remain together, and drawing Johannes aside invited him to return should a severance occur. Meanwhile he arranged for them both to play before the King of Hanover, and gave them an introduction to Liszt at Weimar. But above all he was anxious that Brahms should visit Schumann, to whom he wrote a glowing account of the new star that had appeared so unexpectedly in the musical firmament. As for Johannes, he was overwhelmed by the enthusiasm his music had evoked from one of the leading musicians of Germany, and his excited letter home threw his parents into raptures. They had hoped much for 'Hannes,' but this exceeded their wildest dreams. 'Your great hour has come,' wrote his mother in her reply.

The next move, obviously, must be Weimar. Thanks to Joachim's introduction the two musicians received an invitation from Liszt as soon as they arrived and duly made their way to the Altenburg, where the king of pianists had his home. Liszt received them graciously and introduced them to the gathering of distinguished musicians, all of the neo-German school, that had assembled to meet them. Brahms was too shy to play his compositions in front of Liszt; so his host gently took the manuscripts from him and played, at sight, the E♭ minor Scherzo and part of the C major Sonata. Brahms's admiration knew no bounds. As he said much later in life: 'We others can play the piano, but we all of us have only a few fingers of *his* hands.' Liszt for his part was deeply impressed by Brahms's music. Here was a recruit worth securing for the neo-German school.

Exactly what happened next is not clear. The well-known story of Liszt catching Brahms asleep when he ought to have been listening to the Liszt Sonata is very likely a malicious fabrication of Reményi's.[1] Nor can we say for certain how long Johannes remained in Weimar. What is not in doubt is that he heard a good deal of Liszt's music, and the more he heard the more critical he felt. It is true that his acquaintance with contemporary music was limited, that as yet he knew nothing of Chopin and little of Schumann. But this is not the root of the matter. His instinct for form, his severe training in the school of Marxsen made him acutely conscious of the flimsiness of Liszt's compositions, of the woeful lack of consecutive thought and constructive power which no amount of bright colouring and superficial brilliance could hide. And to these purely aesthetic considerations we must add the whole-hearted repugnance of his straightforward nature to the atmosphere of intrigue with which the Liszt coterie was saturated. He recoiled instinctively. This music was not his music, these ways not his ways. Liszt was aware of his failure to convince and no doubt he regretted it, for his unerring instinct would not fail to divine the potentialities

[1] For a summary of the evidence regarding this episode see Geiringer, *Brahms: his Life and Work.*

that lay in Brahms. Conscious of divergent aims the two men drew apart. There was as yet no open breach; they could and did meet a few months later without any embarrassment. Liszt was too big a man to find in an honest difference of opinion the cause of a quarrel.

It was otherwise with Reményi. He had had quite enough of young Brahms. First at Celle, then at Hanover and now again in Weimar this obscure, unknown pianist had somehow managed to usurp the place in the centre of the stage that rightfully belonged to Reményi. And now, when the mighty Liszt welcomed them with open arms and the brightest of futures seemed dawning, Brahms must needs draw back for the sake of scruples as foolish as they were incomprehensible. Reményi was not going to be so stupid. He made it quite clear to Liszt that he at any rate had found salvation in the neo-German fold, and told Johannes that he had better look after himself.[1]

Somewhat forlorn Johannes betook himself to Göttingen, whither Joachim had gone to attend the university lectures on history and philosophy, and the two young men spent the summer months in each other's company, cementing their friendship and even giving a concert together. With the proceeds of this to support him Johannes went off by himself in August for a walking tour in the Rhine country. He needed solitude. So much had happened since he left Hamburg in April. He had to get his bearings and consider what his next step should be. Joachim was anxious that he should seek out Schumann, who had been fired by Joachim's account and was eager to meet him. But Brahms hesitated. Shyness and modesty held him back, he

[1] We have no concern with Reményi's adventures after he parted from Brahms in 1853. He must have gone to England, for in 1854 he is described as 'violinist to Queen Victoria'—whatever that may mean. Ultimately he died within a year of Brahms, at San Francisco. If we may trust Lawrence Erb (see his *Brahms*) he managed his exit from the world with his usual effectiveness, falling dead on the platform at the conclusion of a solo.

could not forget the fate of the unfortunate package he had sent Schumann in 1850, and perhaps he feared a repetition of the Weimar episode. Meanwhile he was content to wander, and Joachim's visiting-card seemed to open a surprising number of hospitable doors. It was one of these chance visits that ultimately decided him. Herr and Frau Deichmann, with whom he stayed at Mehlem, were Schumann enthusiasts, and Brahms, who knew scarcely anything of Schumann except *Carnaval*, now heard the songs, the piano pieces, the chamber works, and came completely under the spell of 'the most poetic of all day-dreamers.' [1] When he left Mehlem, late in September, he went straight to Düsseldorf and knocked at the door of Robert Schumann.

Schumann had long been expecting him, welcomed him with enthusiasm and after the first greetings were over led him to the piano. Brahms started to play his C major Sonata, but he had not got far when Schumann stopped him in great excitement, exclaiming: 'Clara must hear this!' A moment later he led his wife into the room. 'Now, my dear Clara,' he said, 'you will hear such music as you never heard before; and you, young man, play the piece from the beginning.' It was the Hanover story all over again, but now there was no Reményi to strike a jarring note, and the audience consisted of the leading composer in Germany and the famous pianist who was his wife. Piano pieces, songs, chamber music followed one another. Johannes was asked to stay, and his visit was prolonged from day to day and from week to week. Here at Düsseldorf there was none of the quasi-royal atmosphere of the Altenburg. The Schumanns were simple middle-class folk, sincere, earnest, friendly. In their house Johannes found such a home as before he had scarcely imagined, and in its benign atmosphere his reserve melted and he talked freely of himself, his plans and his dreams. As for the Schumanns, their diaries during this period are filled almost entirely with references to 'the young eagle,' as Schumann called him. How high were the hopes that the elder composer entertained about the

[1] The phrase is Richard Specht's.

13

younger may be seen in a phrase he used in a letter to Joachim written soon after Brahms's arrival: 'This is he that should come.'

One of the most frequent visitors to Schumann's house was Albert Dietrich, a young musician four years Brahms's senior. The two quickly made friends. When Joachim announced that he was coming to Düsseldorf a plot was hatched and a violin Sonata composed, Dietrich writing the first movement, Brahms the scherzo and Schumann an intermezzo and finale. They called it the F.A.E. Sonata after the motto F.A.E. (*Frei aber einsam*, free but solitary) that Joachim had assumed; and when he arrived he had to play the Sonata and guess the composers, all of which he did without the slightest difficulty.[1]

After a happy month with the Schumanns Johannes went to Hanover, whither Joachim had preceded him. Schumann was insistent that he should publish his music and had written to Breitkopf & Härtel at Leipzig, preparing the way; and Brahms was busy giving his works the final touches. But first there was to be another publication of which he knew nothing until he read it with amazement in the *Neue Zeitschrift für Musik* of 28th October. This was Schumann's famous article 'Neue Bahnen' ('New Paths'), one of the most astonishing eulogies a young man of twenty has ever received.

After alluding to the fact that it was now ten years since he had contributed to the paper that once he edited, Schumann glances at the 'many new and significant talents' that have appeared in the interval, citing Joachim, Dietrich, Gade, Franz, Heller and several others (but not any adherent of the neo-German school). Then he goes on:

It seemed to me, who followed the progress of these chosen ones with the greatest interest, that . . . a musician would inevitably appear to whom it was vouchsafed to give the highest and most ideal expression

---

[1] After Brahms's death Joachim, who possessed the manuscript of the Sonata, permitted the publication of the scherzo as a separate piece.

to the tendencies of our time, one who would not show his mastery in a
gradual development, but, like Athena, would spring fully armed from
the head of Zeus. And he has come, a young man over whose cradle
Graces and Heroes stood watch. His name is Johannes Brahms.

There follows an enthusiastic and poetic description of Johannes
playing his own music on the piano, a hope is expressed that 'he
will touch with his magic wand the massed forces of chorus and
orchestra,' and Schumann ends by wishing him God-speed in
the name of his fellow musicians.

'Neue Bahnen' made one thing quite certain: Brahms could
not be ignored. The youth whose virtues had been acclaimed in
such language by such a champion had got to be taken seriously
by every musician in the German-speaking countries. This, no
doubt, was what the generous Schumann intended. But he may
not have realized to what a severe test he was committing his
protégé. No ordinary excellence would be expected from the
subject of such a panegyric. It could be justified only by merit of
an altogether exceptional kind. Furthermore Johannes would
have to reckon with the jealousy of every young composer who
resented the prominence thus suddenly achieved by an upstart
and regarded Schumann's intervention as an unfair advantage for
his rival. Nor were the Liszt faction likely to pass over Schumann's pointed omission of all reference to them. Their hostility
was certain.

With all his gratitude to his benefactor Brahms was by no means
blind to these considerations. His first reaction was to submit
his compositions to a criticism more relentless than ever, and to
destroy a Fantasy Trio and a string Quartet that had been intended
for the publisher. His remaining works he took with him to
Leipzig. Thanks to Schumann's letter and to 'Neue Bahnen'
all went smoothly with Breitkopf & Härtel. As his Op. 1 he
offered them the C major Sonata. It was not his earliest work,
but he considered it his best; and, as he said to a friend, 'when
you show yourself people should see your forehead first.' Besides
this work Breitkopf's accepted two earlier pieces, the F♯ minor

Sonata (Op. 2) and the E♭ minor Scherzo (Op. 4). Op. 3 was a set of songs that included *Liebestreu*. In addition Senff (another publishing house) took a further set of songs (Op. 6) and was to have had a violin Sonata for Op. 5. But somehow or other the manuscript of this got lost, and in its place Brahms let Senff have the F minor piano Sonata, which he had just completed at Hanover.

His business with the publishers did not occupy all his time. He called on Liszt, who was in Leipzig with Berlioz, and was graciously received; and both Liszt and Berlioz were present when, on 17th December, he played his C major Sonata at the Gewandhaus, the stronghold of the Mendelssohn faction. The fact that Brahms could pay such a visit and that Liszt attended the concert makes one doubt whether there had been any serious quarrel at the Altenburg earlier in the year; and it appears that Liszt, whatever he thought of 'Neue Bahnen,' had no grudge against Brahms on that account either. On the whole, indeed, Johannes was well received, though the reviews warned him of what he had to expect. 'Brahms will never become a star of the first magnitude,' wrote one critic; and another wished him 'a speedy deliverance from his over-enthusiastic patrons.'

By Christmas he was back in Hamburg. The modest tour with Reményi had expanded into eight months of wandering, during which the obscure student had been acclaimed by the greatest musicians in the land. His parents had followed his adventures with ever-growing amazement, and Jakob had received a charming letter from the famous Schumann, full of affection and admiration for 'Hannes.' And now here was 'Hannes' himself! They received him with a joy that was mingled with awe—so high had he soared. To them and to all Hamburg the whole story of his Odyssey seemed incredible, some fantastic mistake. Only Marxsen, whom he visited at the first opportunity, was not surprised. Recognition had come to his pupil with uncommon swiftness. But it was no more than his due. As for 'Hannes' himself, he was quite unchanged, unspoilt.

He was full of congratulations when he heard that during his absence his father had been promoted to contrabassist in the theatre orchestra, an appointment that enabled the family to move to somewhat better apartments. It is said too that he made a round of the *Lokale*, flourishing on the piano at each of them to celebrate his emancipation.

## §3. 'STURM UND DRANG' (1853–6)

Early in the new year Johannes went to Hanover to see Joachim. There he found also another friend, Julius Otto Grimm, whom he had met in Leipzig; and the three of them made a happy, careless trio. Before long the Schumanns arrived to hear a performance of Schumann's D minor Symphony, conducted by Joachim. Day succeeded halcyon day. 'Mynheer Domine'[1] was at his best, and the three young men basked in the sunshine radiating from him and from his gracious lady. It was the last of such gatherings and the best.

Schumann had always been a dreamer, and of late he had withdrawn more and more into himself and his dream-world. His habit of long, silent musing had increased, he attended spiritualist séances and believed he had communications from the dead. The devoted Clara viewed these symptoms with distress and was delighted with the renewal of good spirits brought about by congenial company at Hanover. But when the pair returned to Düsseldorf Schumann relapsed alarmingly, and on 27th February the crisis came. For a short time Clara had left him absorbed in composition.[2] Suddenly he rose, quitted the house unnoticed and, clad only in dressing-gown and slippers, made his way to the bridge over the Rhine, from which he threw himself into the

---

[1] This is the nickname by which Schumann was known to his friends.

[2] He is said to have been engaged with variations on the melody in Eb major, which he believed he had received from the spirits of Schubert and Mendelssohn. In 1861 Brahms wrote his own Variations for piano duet on this theme, an act of homage to the dead master.

river. The crew of a Rhine steamer rescued him, and he was brought back—raving. A doctor, hastily called, succeeded in soothing him. But the signs of insanity were patent, and a few days later he was removed to the institution at Endenich, near Bonn, from which he was never to emerge.

Brahms and Joachim at Hanover had their first news of the catastrophe from the newspaper. Aghast and incredulous, they wrote to Dietrich at Düsseldorf for confirmation. It came in a day or two. Tied by his professional duties Joachim could not leave Hanover. But Brahms was free and set off at once to the rescue. He found he was badly needed. Clara, who was with child at the time, had reached the end of her tether. Her husband had already been taken away, and the house was full of kind but foolish women whose efforts to console her were driving her crazy. Johannes began by getting rid of these well-intentioned nuisances and then set to work to steady Clara, who often in later years bore witness to his kindness at this time. The threatened breakdown was averted, and the poor lady rallied her spirits to face the future with fortitude.

Both she and Johannes had need of all their strength during the ordeal of the next two and a half years. Schumann's condition fluctuated. He had periods of complete lucidity, during which he would write charming, perfectly rational letters to Johannes, discussing and appreciating the compositions sent him from time to time by his young friend. Clara too received letters, but not many; and the doctors would not allow her to visit her husband for fear of exciting him. Joachim and Brahms, however, were permitted to see and speak with him occasionally, and sometimes they came back with news of an improvement. But it never lasted. Schumann was suffering from softening of the brain, and by the winter of 1855 it was clear that no hope of his recovery could be entertained.

Only a very strong and very courageous woman could have borne what Clara had to endure. She gradually recovered from the shock of her husband's collapse and after the birth of her son

Felix on 11th June 1854 addressed herself with determination to the task of maintaining her large family. At home there were now seven children to be fed and cared for, and in addition she had to pay the bills from Endenich. She must forget her breaking heart, she must teach, she must play, she must make money by concert tours. It was here that Joachim could help her. They made a splendid team and travelled much together in the winter of 1854–5. Later, in the autumn of 1855, they took Brahms with them—not that they needed a second pianist, but as a tactful means of replenishing his exhausted exchequer. He left them at Danzig to go on by himself, played at Bremen, and on 24th November appeared at one of Otten's concerts in Hamburg. It was his first public appearance in his home town since the days of his studentship, and they listened to him politely but without enthusiasm. Prophets, as we know, are not readily accepted in their own country. But the Hamburgers should not be blamed too much. At Leipzig, where he played in the same year, he was received with a similar coldness. It is easy to lay both failures at the door of jealousy and intrigue, but we shall probably be nearer the truth if we admit an honest bewilderment on the part of the public. The peculiar Brahms blend of romantic warmth with classic strength was something new, and not every audience was gifted with Schumann's imaginative discernment.

But what drove Marxsen and Johannes' other friends almost to despair was not the coolness of his reception, but the rarity of his appearances. Schumann had set all Germany ringing with his name, and it was clearly his business to seize his opportunity and prove in public that his patron had not exaggerated his powers. Yet Johannes was adamant. His place, he felt, was at Clara's side, and as long as she needed him he made Düsseldorf his headquarters.[1] At first loyalty and friendship were his only motives. But soon a warmer feeling was added, and before many months had passed Brahms was deeply in love. It was natural enough.

[1] Dietrich, who might have shared the burden, left to take an appointment at Bonn soon after the beginning of Schumann's illness.

Clara Schumann in her thirty-fifth year still retained the charm that had won so much admiration in her youth. Johannes was twenty-one, young for his age and inexperienced, just in that stage of development when the attraction of an older woman is most strongly felt. Close association did the rest. Of the reality of his sentiments there is no doubt whatever, for they are expressed in his letters for all to see. The 'honoured lady' of 20th July 1854 has become 'my Clara' by 20th June 1855. If we look at the contents of the letters we find him writing as early as 15th December 1854: 'Would to God that I were allowed this day . . . to repeat to you with my own lips that I am dying for love of you.' The letters were mostly written from Düsseldorf, when Clara was away on her concert tours. Her replies are missing. But Johannes would hardly have gone on in this vein with letter after letter if she had sent him any serious rebuke.

An honest love is nothing to be ashamed of. And who shall blame Clara if she accepted the homage of this boyish heart as some small assuagement of her many sorrows, dealt gently with it, perhaps repaid it with an increased warmth of feeling on her own side? Of the actual relations between the two there is no evidence whatever beyond the letters, and a cynical generation cannot be prevented from thinking what it chooses. But those who are familiar with the histories of the honest, idealistic Johannes, the sober, noble-minded Clara, whose whole life was bound up in her husband, those who have read the whole series of letters are not likely to be in doubt. Self-control is not merely a fable, nor are love and innocence incompatible. If further evidence is needed it is to be found in Johannes' enduring devotion to the suffering Robert. He rejoices with Clara whenever her husband's condition shows any improvement, he writes with the most considerate tact when the news from Endenich is bad. On this topic the usually reserved youth shows no shyness whatever, and to the very last he clings to the hope that in the end Schumann will return, sane and whole, to his rejoicing family and friends.

Yet one is often conscious that he had a hard furrow to plough.

In his anxiety to divert Clara's mind from her sorrows he fills his letters with trifling incidents that he hopes will distract her. He has discovered that he is good at jumping; he has bought some tin soldiers which he is sure she will admire; Joachim has been on a visit and smoked a big cigar, after which he was 'very ill, very.' The outlook, the language are often those of a schoolboy, and one is reminded again and again how very young were the shoulders that bore this weight of responsibility. Clara with all her virtues lacked a sense of humour, and sometimes one can see that she has reproved him for his levity. He has no one to advise him, he must do the best he can. He sighs and perseveres.

Publications were few during this trying period. The piano Trio, Op. 8, and probably the Variations on a Hungarian Theme, Op. 21, No. 2, had been begun before Schumann's illness, and these he completed. He also wrote the Variations for piano (Op. 9) on a theme by Schumann and the Ballades (Op. 10). A further set of piano Variations, those in D major (Op. 21, No. 1), were probably composed in 1856. But it is possible that the most significant works of the period never saw the light at all. It is certain that he worked at a symphony. This seems to have been a gloomy affair. He used it later as a sort of quarry, shaping from its opening movement the first movement of the D minor piano Concerto and from its slow movement the funeral march of the Requiem. A piano Quartet in C♯ minor was very likely the origin of the much later Quartet in C minor, Op. 60. This too is dark with the Schumann tragedy. When, after nearly twenty years, he sent the remodelled work to Simrock, his publisher, Brahms wrote: 'You may place a picture on the title-page, namely, a head—with a pistol in front of it. This will give you some idea of the music. I shall send you a photograph of myself for the purpose.' It may have been his dissatisfaction with symphony and quartet in their original form that decided Johannes in 1855 to publish no more for the time being, and work at the improvement of his technique. For a composer whose command of his material was already so superior to that of nearly all his contemporaries to abandon writing for the public for a matter of years is an extraordinary example of self-discipline. In 1856 he started exchanging contrapuntal exercises with Joachim, for whose merits as a technician he always entertained a profound respect.

By the beginning of 1856 Clara was gallantly adjusting herself to her misfortunes. She had faced the prospect of widowhood, was rearranging her life accordingly and no longer needed the constant support of Johannes. This year therefore he spent much more of his time at home in Hamburg. But he and Joachim were both at Bonn in July. For some time Schumann had been sinking. On 27th July Clara, who had been summoned to Endenich, saw her husband for the last time, and on the 29th he died. 'All happiness is gone with his passing,' the poor lady wrote in her diary. She was prostrated and unable to be present at the funeral, which took place at Bonn on the 31st. Brahms and Joachim were chief mourners, and it was Johannes who carried her laurel wreath and laid it on the coffin.

One of the results of Schumann's death was to put an end to Johannes' love-story. Exactly what happened is not known. Did he recoil when the realization of his dreams came in sight at last? Did he suddenly become conscious of the unsuitability of marriage with a lady fourteen years his senior, the widow of a composer more famous by far than he was, herself a pianist of international reputation and the mother of seven children? Or was it Clara's common sense that prevailed, and did she gently indicate to this dearest of friends that her time for love was past? All we can say is that the two of them came to an understanding which, while terminating the idyll, preserved their friendship.

'That it was done abruptly lay in his nature, and perhaps in the nature of the case,' writes Eugenie Schumann many years afterwards. At the time that these events took place Eugenie was too young to know much about them, and we may allow ourselves to believe that this gentle verdict was Clara's own.

On Johannes three years of stress had left their mark. He had found a champion for his music and had lost him; he had met a woman he could love, had wrought valiantly for her and lost her too. There was less of the frank boy about him now. He had begun to erect against the world a barrier of reserve that was to become more impenetrable as he grew older. He had been badly though not mortally hurt, and he determined that never would he offer such hostages to fortune again.

# CHAPTER II

## §1. DETMOLD (1857-9)

THE death of Schumann and the end of his most pressing obligations to Clara [1] left Brahms uncertain of his next step. He had
ideas of making his home at Düsseldorf, at Hamburg, at Hanover,
and discarded them all. Eventually, in the autumn of 1857, he
accepted a post in the little court of Detmold. The prime mover
in this arrangement was a pupil of his, Fräulein Laura von
Meysenbug, sister of the Detmold chamberlain. Laura succeeded
in interesting the Princess Friederike in the young composer,
Brahms was invited for a preliminary visit at Whitsuntide 1857,
and this proving satisfactory he returned in September for a more
extended engagement that lasted till New Year. The invitation
was repeated and again accepted for the same period in the two
following years.

Detmold was a sleepy, old-fashioned town, situated in magnificent forest country, where Johannes could indulge his love of
walking to his heart's content. Its centre was the court of the
reigning prince, which had succeeded in preserving some of the
charm as well as much of the strict etiquette of the eighteenth
century. Brahms was never at his best on formal occasions, and
his uncouthness did not go unobserved. But his youth, his
capacity for friendship and his unmistakable genius carried him
through. Even when, at a rehearsal of the choir, its conductor
appeared without his tie the ladies of the court overlooked the

---

[1] Clara never ceased to be a factor in Johannes' life. But after the
events described in the last chapter she withdrew, perhaps deliberately,
from the centre of the stage. In 1857 she left Düsseldorf with all her
family and took up a teaching appointment in Berlin.

omission, and he himself only discovered it when he came to undress at night. Besides conducting the choral society he was expected to play at court concerts and to teach the piano to Princess Friederike. She proved a diligent and accomplished pupil, and a real affection sprang up between her and Brahms, whose snort of approval after she had performed at a concert was the applause she liked best to hear. Moreover her patronage ensured him a plentiful supply of rich and distinguished lady pupils who paid well and thus made up for the smallness of his official salary. Nor did he lack congenial company. Karl Bargheer, the leader of the court orchestra, was an old acquaintance as well as an excellent violinist; and he struck up a warm friendship with Karl von Meysenbug, a nephew of Fräulein Laura.

The most characteristic compositions of these Detmold visits are the two orchestral Serenades (Op. 11 in D major and Op. 16 in A major), whose very titles conjure up memories of Mozart and the eighteenth century. A more considerable work, the piano Concerto in D minor, carries no whisper of the peaceful haven in which Brahms's spirit was slowly recovering after the buffetings of the preceding years, but takes us straight back to the stressful period of Schumann's illness. The origin of the first movement is to be sought, as we have seen, in an earlier, abandoned symphony; and though the other movements may have been written later, the inscription above the second, 'Benedictus qui venit in nomine Domini,'[1] makes it clear that Schumann was still in his mind. Joachim conducted the first public performance of the Concerto at Hanover on 22nd January 1859, with the composer at the piano. It was received respectfully, though without enthusiasm. But a few days later, on 27th January, when he played it at the Leipzig Gwandhaus (Rietz conducting) Brahms

---

[1] Brahms wrote these words in Joachim's copy of the score. The fact that he afterwards struck his pen through them shows only that he changed his mind about leaving on record this clue to his mood and does not affect the import of the clue itself with its obvious reference to Schumann's nickname.

sustained the most decisive defeat of his career. The performance was excellent, as he admits in a letter to Joachim. It was the Concerto itself that did not please. He looks squarely at that fact and puts a bold face on it as he continues (with a probably unconscious echo of Beethoven): 'It will come to please one day when I have improved the shape of its body. . . . I believe this is the best thing that could happen to any one. . . . After all I am still trying and groping. All the same the hissing was rather too much.' Control himself as he may, the disappointment has been bitter and the young lip quivers. Not till the splendid performance at Mannheim under Hermann Levi (with Brahms at the piano) in 1865 can the Concerto be said to have won real appreciation.

Perhaps it was the encouragement of Bargheer, combined with the opportunities at Detmold for instrumental performance, that turned the thoughts of Johannes once more to chamber music. Although he had certainly composed pieces in this *genre* during the years of stress, nothing had reached the publisher since the Trio, Op. 8; and even now he was not quite ready to face the critics again. His habit of keeping a new work by him for constant revision, and of saying nothing about it till he was finally satisfied, makes it difficult to say exactly what was written at Detmold and what was not. But the G minor piano Quartet, Op. 25, was certainly tried over by Bargheer and his associates in 1859, and a beginning was very likely made with the B♭ major Sextet, Op. 18, the piano Quintet, Op. 34, and even the G major Sextet, Op. 36. There is indeed a quotation from the last-named work in a letter to Clara Schumann as early as 7th February 1855, although it was not published till 1866.

On the whole Brahms had good reason to be grateful to Detmold. He had leisure to study, to broaden the basis of his art, and he learnt to become a good choral conductor. Above all he slowly recovered his serenity in these quiet and beautiful surroundings. True, the place was a backwater. He was bored and irritated by the court routine and the limited horizons, intellectual and musical, of most of his pupils, and when the coming of each new year released him from his obligations he was always in haste to be away. In 1860 he refused the invitation to resume his appointment. He was probably right. The time had come when he must face the world once more with his music. But that he could do so with a steady heart and high courage he owed in no small degree to Detmold.

## §2. GÖTTINGEN (1858–9)

Labels are useful things, and it is convenient to refer to the years 1857–9 as the Detmold period in Brahms's life. But the phrase becomes misleading if we forget that he was at Detmold only for three months or a little more at the end of each year. For the rest of the time Hamburg was his headquarters, as it had been ever since the death of Schumann. But before embarking on some account of his doings in Hamburg we will glance at two episodes that have no connection with his home town. Each of these in its way throws a light on his character.

In the summer of 1858 Johannes spent part of his holiday at Göttingen. Clara was there, on a visit from Berlin; and he was happy to find also Julius Otto Grimm, his old friend of the Hanover days in 1854. Before long, however, a new interest began to occupy him. Agathe von Siebold was the daughter of a professor of medicine and the possessor of a fine soprano voice. Very likely it was her voice that first attracted Johannes, for she was not particularly beautiful. It was now nearly two years since he had come to his final understanding with Clara, and there is nothing astonishing in his yielding to the fascinations of Agathe, who, on her side, was by no means indifferent to him. Nor, on the other hand, need we be surprised that Clara, seeing how the land lay, was human enough to leave Göttingen suddenly in something like a huff. Johannes stayed on till his duties recalled him to Detmold, and returned as soon as he was free to do so at the beginning of 1859. For a while the path of true love ran smoothly, and we probably owe to Agathe many of the songs Opp. 14 and 19, including *Vor dem Fenster* and *Der Schmied*.

But it was difficult to keep a secret in a small town like Göttingen. The time came when Grimm felt bound to warn Johannes that he and Agathe were getting themselves talked about. Unless he wished to compromise her he must stop seeing her—or announce their engagement. Although the pair had already exchanged rings in secret Johannes was startled to find the crisis already upon him and shied away like a frightened colt. His constitutional fear of losing his freedom was reinforced on this occasion by the consciousness that his position in his profession was still insecure, that struggles, humiliations even, might still await him. 'If she had wanted to comfort me,' he wrote many years afterwards to his friend Widmann, 'a wife to pity her husband for his non-success —ugh!' Under the stress of these emotions he wrote Agathe one of the most extraordinary letters that ever sprang even from his pen. 'I love you! I must see you again!' he says, 'but I cannot wear fetters. Write to me whether I am to come back, to take you in my arms.' What was the poor girl to make of that? She answered, breaking off the engagement, nor was it till her old age that she found it in her heart to forgive him. Johannes was uneasily aware that he had not come very creditably out of the affair. 'I have played the scoundrel towards Agathe,' he said, and enshrined the musical letters of her name in the G major Sextet with some vague idea of making amends and salving his conscience. Whether this pious act was any consolation to Agathe is not on record.

## §3. THE MANIFESTO (1860)

Nearly all Brahms's mistakes in life were in the conduct of his private affairs. His career he managed on the whole with wisdom and discretion. But there is one exception: his dealings with Liszt and the neo-German school. The story of his going to sleep at the Altenburg in 1853 while Liszt was playing may be a fabrication of Reményi's; but it gained currency and made Brahms look a fool and a boor. Liszt's magnanimous attitude heightened the impression, and Johannes soon found himself in a false position. His dislike of Liszt's music was perfectly sincere and, from the point of view of his own art, reasonable. But if he gave expression to it he was liable to be suspected of personal animus. Worse still, the animus was there. He came almost to hate the man whose ideals he believed to be false but who always contrived somehow to put him in the wrong. In the end his feelings overruled his judgment and led him into the most serious blunder he ever made.

To understand things properly we must go back a bit. In 1834 Schumann started the *Neue Zeitschrift für Musik*, a progressive organ that fought the battle of the young romantics against the more narrow-minded supporters of an older tradition, Schumann's 'Philistines.' One of the Philistine strongholds was at Leipzig where Mendelssohn was king by right of genius. But though a good king he was a bad Philistine and on the most friendly and sympathetic terms with the 'Band of David' across the frontier. His death in 1847 was a great misfortune, for with it Leipzig relapsed into an arid conservatism that was suspicious of everything new.

Meanwhile a new party was arising headed by Liszt and Wagner, the neo-German party, as it presently styled itself. Liszt, basing himself on such things as Mendelssohn's overtures and Berlioz's *Symphonie Fantastique*, was evolving the symphonic poem. Wagner was exiled from Germany in 1849, and his most characteristic works were still to be written. But it was already evident that his ideas for opera were at least as revolutionary as Liszt's for the symphony. In 1844 Schumann resigned the editorship of the *Neue Zeitschrift* and was succeeded in 1845 by Paul Brendel, an enthusiastic neo-German; so that the paper became the organ of the new school. To begin with, the antagonism between the factions was limited to artistic matters. Joachim, the friend and protégé of Mendelssohn, was warmly welcomed by the neo-Germans when he came into their camp after Mendelssohn's death; and in spite of the Altenburg episode Brendel had been conspicuously fair to Brahms. A long essay that appeared in the *Zeitschrift* in 1855 made an honest effort to understand the aims of Schumann's young prophet, and the paper's review of the D minor Concerto after the Leipzig fiasco of 1859 was kinder than that of any other journal.

Not all the neo-Germans were as fair-minded as Brendel, and the party was definitely not pleased when Joachim, in the early 1850s, showed a tendency to withdraw from their faction and attach himself to the Schumanns. Schumann himself had never accepted the neo-German creed; Clara had little admiration for Liszt's compositions and was openly hostile to Wagner's. Then Brahms appeared, and in spite of assiduous neo-German wooing went the same way as Joachim. After Schumann's disappearance from the musical stage in 1854 Johannes, Clara, Joachim, Dietrich and a few others found themselves occupying an independent position somewhere between the Leipzig conservatives and the Weimar group of neo-Germans. Relations with Weimar gradually worsened. Liszt, for all his magnanimity, never played a Brahms work in public. Hans von Bülow, one of his satellites, started by showing an interest in the young Hamburger, and his performance of part of the C major Sonata early in 1854 is actually the first recorded instance of a Brahms work being played at a concert by someone other than the composer. But he too cooled off—though not, as things turned out, for ever. On the other side Joachim identified himself more and more closely with the Schumann–Brahms group. He had no personal quarrel with Liszt. But he came to see that Liszt's aims and methods were not his, and in 1857 he wrote him a courteous, straightforward letter admitting as much and withdrawing from the neo-Germans altogether. Liszt maintained a dignified silence; but his followers may not have been entirely wrong in attributing Joachim's defection to the influence of Brahms, whose hostility to their movement was by this time well known. By 1859 things had got to such a pitch that when the *Zeitschrift* celebrated its twenty-fifth birthday at Zwickau, the birthplace of its founder (Schumann), neither Schumann's widow nor his two closest friends were invited to the festivities.

What particularly enraged Brahms in the propaganda of the *Zeitschrift* was the calm assumption that the neo-German theories were now accepted by all musicians of consequence; and at the beginning of 1860 he proposed to Joachim that they should issue a manifesto protesting against this point of view. In the absence of any specific attack by the neo-Germans Joachim considered such a challenge ill advised, but he allowed Brahms to over-rule him. The document was drawn up and all Germany canvassed for signatures. Many of these were promised, but only four musicians had actually signed when by some means un-explained the manifesto found its way into the office of the Berlin *Echo* and was forthwith published. It ran:

The undersigned have long followed with regret the pursuits of a certain party, whose organ is Brendel's *Zeitschrift für Musik*.

The above journal continually spreads the view that musicians of more serious endeavour are fundamentally in accord with the tendencies it represents, that they recognize in the compositions by the leaders of this group works of artistic value and that altogether, and especially in north Germany, the contentions for and against the so-called music of the future are concluded, and the dispute settled in its favour.

To protest against such a misrepresentation of facts is regarded as their duty by the undersigned, and they declare that, so far at least as they are concerned, the principles stated by Brendel's journal are not recognized, and that they regard the productions of the leaders and pupils of the so-called 'New German' school, which in part simply reinforce these principles in practice and in part again enforce new and unheard-of theories, as contrary to the innermost spirit of music, strongly to be deplored and condemned.

JOHANNES BRAHMS.
JOSEPH JOACHIM.
JULIUS OTTO GRIMM.
BERNHARD SCHOLZ.[1]

---

[1] Translation by Eric Blom in Richard Specht's *Johannes Brahms*.

Even with the many additional signatures its authors had intended to obtain this would strike one as a singularly maladroit document. Who were Brahms and his friends to lay down the law about what was and what was not 'the innermost spirit of music'? As things were, the manifesto went off with all the devastating effect of a damp squib. Musical Germany merely laughed at the presumption of four young men who took it upon them to rebuke their betters. Liszt made no answer whatsoever. Wagner had less self-restraint. His retort, published anonymously in the *Zeitschrift*, was the venomous, anti-Semitic *Das Judentum in der Musik*, with its spiteful shafts aimed at Joachim.

But the chief sufferer from his folly was Brahms himself. He had yielded to an impulse and he lived to regret it. Henceforth, he resolved, suppression should be his rule. Never again would he allow his instincts to escape from his iron self-control. On the whole he stuck to that determination, and his life and his music are the poorer. In the world of music he had cut himself off irretrievably from the progressive group. He refused to join the conservative Leipzig faction and preserved his independence. But having laid down the law he must keep it himself. The luxuriance of his earliest manner he had already pruned considerably. Now comes a more ruthless austerity, an increased reserve, an even sterner rejection of the picturesque for its own sake. He entrenches himself more firmly than ever behind the well-tried ramparts of classical design. The Handel Variations are a magnificent assertion of the new attitude, virile, dignified, full of creative vigour. But when one looks at the songs or at the piano pieces of his latest years, when time had hushed the loud sounds of conflict, one wonders what might have happened if that other, genial Brahms, whom circumstances compelled to flagellate himself so unmercifully in 1860, had escaped that cruel repression.

With Wagner he had started a lifelong feud, a feud that every music-lover must regret; though if they had not fallen out over the manifesto they would very likely have done so over something else, for their aims were different and both were intolerant.

Wagner's attacks on Brahms were frequent and sometimes vitriolic. Brahms forbore to reply in print; he had learnt that he was unhandy with words. But in his letters and conversations he often betrayed his antipathy to Wagner's personality, an antipathy that led him once or twice into petty acts of malice his friends can only deplore.

Wagner was far too good a musician to be blind to the merits of Brahms's works, heartily though he disliked their creator. On the only occasion when they met—at Penzing, early in 1863?—Brahms is said to have played his Handel Variations. Wagner was impressed. 'This shows,' he said, 'what may still be done with the old forms provided that someone appears who knows how to treat them.'[1] Brahms's acquaintance with Wagner's music began before 1860, and from the very first he felt for it a temperamental aversion that never left him and often found expression when he was talking or writing to his friends. But he too could recognize genius. Specht goes too far when he asserts that Brahms never said a disrespectful word about Wagner. But in his later years he was a constant attendant at the opera on Wagner nights; and when one day Heuberger remarked to him that 'Wagner must be held chiefly responsible for the confusion prevailing in the heads of us young people,' he flared up and replied: 'Nonsense! The *misunderstood* Wagner has done it. Those understand *nothing* of the real Wagner who are led astray by him. Wagner's is one of the clearest heads that ever existed in the world.'[2] The news of Wagner's death was brought to him at a choral rehearsal. At once he closed his score. 'A master is dead,' he told the singers. 'To-day we sing no more.'

## §4. HAMBURG (1856–62)

When he was not at Detmold or Göttingen, when he was not visiting his scattered friends or fulfilling concert engagements,

[1] The evidence for this anecdote is not conclusive.

[2] This anecdote is quoted by Florence May from an article by Heuberger in *Die Musik*.

Brahms spent most of his time during the years 1856–62 at Hamburg. At first he stayed with his parents, for whom his affection was undiminished. But at the beginning of 1858, finding his narrow quarters at home inconvenient and having, it must be supposed, some money from Detmold in his pocket, he moved out to the suburb of Hamm, where he established himself as a boarder with Frau Dr. Rösing (to whom he subsequently dedicated the piano Quartet in A major). One day he heard two girls singing in a neighbouring garden, made their acquaintance, roped in two more girls, and formed the four of them into a vocal quartet, which he much enjoyed coaching.

Next year his ideas expanded. He began by 'borrowing' a choir of girls' voices that he had heard at a wedding, added the quartet of 1858, and ended by forming the Hamburg Ladies' Choir. It started with twenty-eight voices, but soon swelled to forty. From this body of singers, whom he trained without any remuneration, Brahms derived profound satisfaction. He wrote of them ecstatically to Clara, and was immensely pleased when that lady, on a visit to Hamburg, attended a rehearsal and inscribed her name in the book of members. One obvious necessity for such a society was a set of rules, and Brahms supplied one that still makes amusing reading, signing it 'Johannes Kreisler, junior.'[1] At first he had little of his own that he could give his girls to sing. But he soon supplemented the *Ave Maria* (Op. 12), composed at Detmold in 1858, with other pieces for women's voices, and before the choir was disbanded in 1862 (owing to his own move to Vienna) he had provided it with quite a respectable repertory. That there should be a sentimental element in the business was only to be expected. Johannes seems to have thought a good deal about one of his singers, Bertha Porubszky,

[1] Kreisler is a fictitious character of E. T. A. Hoffmann's, whose name Brahms adopted in his early student days, probably before he knew that Schumann had celebrated Kreisler in his *Kreisleriana*. Throughout his early life he copied passages that struck him in the authors he read into a diary he called 'The Young Kreisler's Treasure-Chest.'

a visitor from Vienna. But once more it all came to nothing. Bertha went back to Vienna where she soon afterwards married Arthur Faber. However, she retained Brahms's friendship, and he celebrated the birth of her first-born with the best-known of all his songs, the *Wiegenlied*. No other member of the choir stepped into Bertha's place. But he was fond of them all, and when, after his departure to Detmold in 1859, they clubbed together to present him with a handsome silver inkstand he was delighted.

All this while his reputation was steadily growing. He was ever an industrious composer, and in 1860 he revoked the self-denying ordinance imposed during Schumann's illness, and once more allowed his work to reach the publisher. It is not enough, however, for a man to publish his compositions. He must, especially if his music be serious in intent and individual in expression, ensure that it is frequently and adequately performed. Brahms was rapidly establishing his own position as a first-rate pianist and at least an adequate conductor. But this alone would scarcely have been sufficient to keep him in the public eye, and he was exceptionally fortunate in enlisting the help of three artists already famous, whose united talents could do justice to almost the whole of his output. For the piano music there was Clara Schumann, who had already begun her lifelong evangel on behalf of Johannes and her husband. The orchestral music, as well as the chamber music, was in the trustworthy hands of Joachim in his double capacity of conductor and violinist. There remained the songs, of which the number was already considerable. For these Brahms had found a noble and sensitive interpreter in Julius Stockhausen, whose acquaintance he had made in 1855. Stockhausen's big reputation had been made by his singing of Schubert [1] and Schumann. Now he took to Brahms's songs with enthusiasm and never lost an opportunity of singing them, if possible with the composer at the piano.

Yet all these advantages failed to secure Brahms the recognition

[1] He is said to have been the first ever to sing the *Schöne Müllerin* songs as a complete cycle.

he longed to obtain from the city of his birth. Already in 1861 it was evident that the ageing Grund, conductor of the Hamburg Philharmonic Society, would not be able much longer to fulfil his duties, and there is little doubt that Brahms prolonged his residence in Hamburg till 1862 and refused various tempting offers to migrate elsewhere in the hope of being appointed his successor. His associations with the town, his position in the world of music and the enthusiastic support of Joachim all gave him grounds for confidence; so that his disappointment was all the keener when the time came and he found himself passed over for Stockhausen who, whatever his gifts as a singer, had nothing like the qualifications of Johannes for a post of this kind. In a letter to Clara Schumann of 18th November 1862 he declares his rejection to be 'a much sadder event for me than you can imagine. I am as much attached to my native town' (he goes on) 'as I might be to my mother . . . and now this hostile friend comes and ousts me.' It is very much to his credit that he said nothing of all this to Stockhausen, and that their friendship was not marred.

His letter to Clara he writes from Vienna. In spite of the pleasure he derived from his ladies' choir and the society of his parents he had long been chafing at the circumstances that kept him in Hamburg when he might have been pursuing his career so much more effectively elsewhere. Now the chain that bound him was broken, and he felt that he must get away at once from the scene of his disappointment. It was a change he wanted. Where he went mattered little, and his decision to visit Vienna was made almost casually. Vienna was the most famous of all musical centres; he must certainly go there some time. Clara Schumann and Joachim, it so happened, had both been pressing him recently to make the trip. Why not now? He packed up his things and on 8th September 1862 he set out. That he was going to a new home where he would spend the rest of his life never crossed his mind.

His parents were somewhat of an anxiety to him. Already

for some time he had been contributing to the upkeep of their home out of his increasing but still slender resources. That allowance would continue. But he knew his father's rashness in money matters and provided against an unforeseen economic crisis in his own way. 'Dear father,' he said just before his departure, 'if things go badly with you the best consolation is always in music. Read carefully in my old *Saul* and you'll find what you want.' The enigmatic advice puzzled old Jakob, but when the difficult time arrived he remembered it, took the score of *Saul* from the shelf, opened it, and found between the pages a substantial supply of bank-notes.

# CHAPTER III

## THE VIENNESE MASTER

### §1. RISING FAME (1862–8)

THE Vienna to which Brahms came in September 1862 was a city with a musical tradition unrivalled in Europe. Here Mozart had lived and worked through the last part of his short life. Through these streets he had been carried to his unknown grave. That was in 1791, seventy-one years before. In 1862 there would be very few left who had seen him alive. But more would remember Haydn, who died in Vienna in 1809; and there were many people still in late middle life who had seen and spoken to Beethoven and Schubert.[1] With Schubert the line of Viennese giants came to an end. But the traditions they had created survived and flourished, and Vienna still drew musical talent from all over the Continent. Karl Goldmark was already settled there when Brahms arrived, and for Johann Strauss Vienna was birthplace as well as home. Many of those composers who did not even belong to the city had paid it a visit. Schumann had made a romantic pilgrimage to the graves of Beethoven and Schubert, Liszt had played to Vienna audiences. But the most interesting stranger in 1862 was Richard Wagner, who was much in the capital from 1861 to 1864, busy with his plans for the production of *Tristan*—plans that ultimately proved abortive.

If, as a result of this plethora of distinguished musicians, added to their own natural gaiety, the Viennese were somewhat light-minded (as Mozart, Schubert and even Beethoven had found in their time), at least they were less faction-ridden than the citizens of other musical centres. Leipzig stood for Mendelssohn, Weimar for Liszt, with a tendency to look coldly on any one who

[1] Beethoven died in 1827, Schubert in 1828, both in Vienna.

was out of sympathy with their special hero. But Vienna was perfectly ready to applaud Mendelssohn on Monday, Liszt on Tuesday, Mozart on Wednesday, Schumann on Thursday and Wagner on Friday, and before long it was to show that it still had Saturday free for Brahms. First, however, he must prove himself. The Viennese had heard of Schumann's young prophet; but in spite of all those assiduous propagandists, Clara Schumann and Joachim, had been able to do they still knew very little of either the man or his music.

Having established himself in modest bachelor lodgings he began to look round. One of his first calls was on his old Hamburg flame Bertha Faber (as she now was) and her husband. His feeling for Bertha had already cooled to disinterested friend¬ ship, and with her and her Arthur he entered into a cordial relationship that lasted till his death. Then there was Karl Grädener, whom he had known in Hamburg. Grädener had left his Hamburg vocal academy and was now a teacher at the Vienna Conservatoire. Luise Dustmann, the soprano, he had met a few months earlier on a flying visit to Cologne, and it is possible that his susceptible heart was for a while not indifferent to her personal charms. Just now Luise had her anxieties, for Wagner desired to cast her for Isolde, a part whose difficulties were already legendary, even before the production of the opera. But her Wagnerian preoccupations did not prevent her from taking an in¬ terest in Brahms, of whose songs she was an admirable interpreter.

Other links were soon forged. Julius Epstein, bearded pianist and teacher, with his inexhaustible kindness and 'resounding *adagio* laugh,'[1] was clearly destined to take his place in the Brahms circle. He lived in the house where Mozart had composed *Figaro*, and it was there that Brahms's piano Quartets in G minor and A major, now finally completed, were tried over for the first time. The first violin was Hellmesberger, leader of the best quartet in Vienna. Hellmesberger was enraptured. 'This,' he cried, 'is Beethoven's heir'; and it was his and Epstein's combined

[1] The phrase is Specht's, who knew him.

enthusiasm that led to the first public performance of the G minor Quartet at Hellmesberger's concert on 16th November, with the composer at the piano. The work was coldly received, one critic going so far as to call it 'an offence against the laws of style.' But Epstein was undaunted and went on to arrange a special Brahms concert on the 29th, brushing aside the composer's hesitations. This time the same team played the A major Quartet, which was little more successful than its predecessor, though Brahms won some praise with the Handel Variations, which were also on the programme. But Vienna showed singular generosity in giving him a hearing. The concert on 10th April 1863, when he conducted some of his choruses for female voices, was at least the fifth at which his music had been performed. Both the orchestral Serenades had been played, as well as the F minor piano Sonata, and Marie Wilt had sung some of the songs.

Among the audience who listened to the F minor Sonata and the songs on 6th January were two men whose quarrel was later to become famous, Wagner and Hanslick, the critic of the Vienna *Presse*.[1] Hanslick's successive criticisms of Brahms's music are probably fairly typical of Viennese opinion. His notice of the performance of the A major Quartet on 29th November 1862 is definitely adverse, though free from malice. But a few days later (on 3rd December) he hedges and says it is still too early to pronounce judgment. After the concert of 6th January he professes himself genuinely pleased with the slow movement of the F minor Sonata and hopes Brahms will not leave Vienna, where he has made so many friends 'as man and artist.' Perhaps the final stage of his conversion was effected by the performance of the A major Serenade on 8th March, which drew from him the assertion that the composer was rapidly developing into a true master. From that time onward Brahms could always count on support and encouragement from Hanslick.

[1] Hanslick's anti-Wagnerian fury did not rise to its full height till a few years later. Wagner retorted by 'guying' Hanslick as Beckmesser in *Meistersinger*.

If the appearance of a new masterpiece was not always greeted with unstinting praise the defect lay in Hanslick's limited sensibility. The critic of the *Presse* wielded a graceful, sometimes a brilliant pen; his judgment was cool, his writing logical and his influence on musical opinion considerable. But he had no depth. The later Beethoven he regarded as decadent, he was impervious to the greater works of Bach and could make nothing of Palestrina. What wonder then that he reviled Wagner just as he afterwards reviled Bizet and Richard Strauss? What wonder that in 1885, after listening for the first time to the opening movement of Brahms's E minor Symphony (played, it must be admitted, as a two-piano duet), the poor old feather-head sighed and said: 'You know, I had the feeling that two enormously clever people were cudgelling one another'?

Brahms was perfectly well aware of Hanslick's limitations. As early as 1856 he tells Clara Schumann that he has had to give up the attempt to read a book of Hanslick's because it contained 'such a number of stupid things.' Hanslick's anti-Wagnerian campaign enraged him. 'I shall have to be called a Wagnerian,' he writes to Joachim in 1863, 'chiefly of course for the disagreement that must be provoked in any reasonable human being by the manner in which musicians here attack him.' Much later in life his answer to a remark made by the composer Josef Labor showed that his opinion of Hanslick was substantially the same. Labor observed that Johann Strauss in his waltzes never made the second part thematically dependent on the first. This odd criticism of the waltz king produced the reply: 'That would be to ask from Hanslick the science of Spitta and Chrysander.[1]

Yet Brahms had not been many months in Vienna before he and Hanslick were fast friends; and the years only drew them closer together. Brahms was no sycophant to toady to the powerful critic, and we might be at a loss to account for his devotion

[1] I have this anecdote from Mr. Paul Wittgenstein, a pupil of Labor's. Spitta and Chrysander were two musicologists whose scholarship was beyond question.

had he not himself supplied the easy explanation. Right at the end of his life, in 1895, he wrote to Clara Schumann:

I cannot help it, but I know few men for whom I feel such a hearty attachment as I do for him [Hanslick]. To be as simple, good, bene-volent, honourable, serious and modest and everything else as I know him to be I regard as something very beautiful and rare. . . . And I am all the more entitled to proclaim his immense ability in his own sphere, seeing that we each have such very different points of view.

It was during this first winter in Vienna that Brahms received the news of Joachim's engagement to a contralto singer, Amalie Weiss. He hastened to congratulate his old friend, whose good fortune naturally set him thinking of his own situation. 'I have not ceased to wonder,' he says, 'whether, since I must guard against dreams of another kind, I had better not experience and enjoy everything with one exception, or whether I should not make sure of one thing—that is, go home and let the rest slide.' It is an obscure utterance, full of hints and allusions that are susceptible of more than one interpretation. The writer's eager-ness to confide to his beloved 'Jussuf' the secrets of his heart is clear enough. But the boyish candour of 1853 has been overlaid by a crust of reserve he cannot break. Every instinct of his re-pressed nature protests against confession, distorting the sentence into so cryptic a shape as to thwart his intention. The thoughts of a young bachelor regarding marriage are often mixed and some-times a little disingenuous; but they can seldom have been clothed in phrases quite so oblique as these. Unfortunately this tendency to obscurity was only the symptom of an inner withdrawal that grew with the years. It clouded the simplest affairs, extended even to his business correspondence and played its part in many of the quarrels that marred the peacefulness of his days and cost him many good friends. Yet he, who so frequently misunderstood the communications of others, finding offence where no real cause for it existed, was curiously blind to the ambiguities of his own language and constantly dismayed by its disastrous effects. In the end he gave up and allowed many a passing disagreement to develop into a serious breach merely for want of the straightforward letter that would have put matters right. He had learnt that the straightforward letter was beyond his powers to indite.

Happily his congratulations to Joachim, whatever their literary deficiencies, left no doubt regarding the cordiality of his sentiments. As soon as the Vienna season was over he went himself to Hanover to pay his respects to Amalie in person. He found not only a very charming lady, but a remarkable artist. None, save Stock~ hausen alone, could so enter into the spirit of his songs, none could so fire his genius as Amalie Joachim. The Alto Rhapsody, which she interpreted as no one else could, is only the greatest of many works that owe much of their inspiration to her.

From May to August Brahms was in Hamburg, where he took new lodgings and prepared, it seemed, to settle down again. It was not a happy time for him. Even before his departure for Vienna there had been signs that his father and mother, after so many years together, no longer understood each other as before. Their disagreements had been one of his reasons for moving to Hamm. Now they were openly at odds, and their other children made no effort to reconcile them. Fritz Brahms stood aloof and did nothing, Elise sided passionately with her mother against her father; so that it fell to Johannes to play the peacemaker. It was a task he hated, for he loved them both, but he did his best and actually succeeded in patching up a truce. It was, however, with a heavy and foreboding heart that he left Hamburg to spend a few days at Baden, where Clara Schumann had recently taken a house,[1] and then go on to Vienna.

Several reasons had combined to bring about this change ol plan. With quarrels at home and Stockhausen in the coveted post at the Philharmonic Hamburg had become definitely dis~ tasteful. Vienna, on the other hand, held out a positive attraction, the directorship of its *Singakademie* (Academy of Singing), which had been offered to him in the spring. The proposal flattered,

[1] Baden was the home of Clara and her family from 1863 to 1874. She took a house in the Lichtenthal suburb.

pleased and worried him all at the same time. He longed for the security of a regular post, and perhaps he was even more anxious to show the Hamburgers that he could get on without them. At the same time, however, he was jealous for his personal independence. There was an interval while these conflicting motives fought within him—and then he accepted. His decision brought him little satisfaction. The Academy of Singing lacked vitality and enthusiasm, and even the new conductor could not arrest its decline. He took office on 28th September, and for a few weeks his energy galvanized the choir into a semblance of keenness. Then they relapsed, discouraged by the number of new works, especially the difficult and unfamiliar Bach cantatas, that their new director expected them to learn. Perhaps the most successful concert was the fourth, an all-Brahms programme, wherein some motets and a folksong arrangement won favourable comment, though the instrumental numbers went unnoticed.[1] When the season came to an end in May 1864 Brahms found himself anything but content with the results achieved and inclined to attribute some of the blame to his own deficiencies as conductor. Having reached this conclusion he resigned. It was a disappointment, no doubt. But was it not also, perhaps, something of a relief?

In June he was back in Hamburg, where his father had achieved the summit of his modest ambitions, having been appointed by Stockhausen to one of the double-bass desks in the Philharmonic orchestra. Ironically enough this very success had caused a fresh outbreak of the family quarrel. Jakob's new duties

[1] Concerning one of these pieces, the B♭ major Sextet, Brahms could afford to be philosophical, since the Hellmesberger combination had gained a resounding success with it at a concert on 27th December 1863. The other, a Sonata for two pianos in F minor, which the composer played with Karl Tausig, was a recasting of a work originally written for string quintet (with two cellos). Its failure to please on this occasion may have had something to do with its final metamorphosis into the piano Quintet, Op. 34.

compelled him to practise on his instrument more regularly and assiduously than he had done for some time. That the continual grunting should cause some distress to his wife and daughter is not surprising. But they took rather an extreme step when they banished him to an uncomfortable attic. Johannes arrived to find that the wounds he had tried so hard to heal had broken out afresh, and this time there was no help for it but separation. The home was broken up, Jakob going to No. 80 Grosse Bleichen, the two women to rooms in the Lange Reihe. Throughout the whole dreary business it was Johannes who had to take the initiative, make and carry out the plans. His brother and sister gave him no help. Yet he made no complaint, doing what was needful with a heavy heart. The new arrangement meant fresh demands upon his purse, for the resources of the old people were not equal to the demands of two establishments. Johannes was still a poor man, but he shouldered the responsibility and spoke of it to no one.

It was not to last very long. After visiting Baden he drifted back in the autumn to Vienna. There, at the beginning of February 1865, he received a telegram calling him urgently to his mother's bedside. He hastened at once to Hamburg, but arrived too late. Johanna had died from a stroke. Brahms was inconsolable, for his love for his mother went to the very roots of his nature. But there was nothing he could do, and after the funeral he returned to Vienna and his work, saying little to any one and bearing his troubles, as usual, alone. A warm-hearted letter of sympathy from Clara reached him in Vienna. It was the best sort of consolation he could have, and he replies gratefully:

Your letter made me feel near you, just as one wishes to be near one's friends at such times. . . . When once this sad year is over I shall begin to miss my dear good mother ever more and more.

Another of the links binding him to Hamburg, and that the strongest of all, had snapped.

Brahms's pen was busy in 1865, though his habit of keeping his compositions for a long time on the stocks and of guarding his secret till it was ready for publication makes it hard to be certain at what date a particular piece was actually composed. Thus the Waltzes for piano duet, which were finished in January (before his mother's death), and were dedicated to Hanslick,[1] had been accumulating for several years. Some of them (thinks Florence May) date back to Detmold. The publication of the F minor piano Quintet marked the end of a long series of adventures for that work, and the G major Sextet (the 'Agathe' Sextet), which was finished in May, goes back in part at least to 1855, when Johannes quoted the opening bars of the *Adagio* in a letter to Clara. Other works completed this year were the E minor cello Sonata (Op. 38) and the horn Trio, in whose slow movement Specht hears the composer's lament for his dead mother; and Brahms devoted a lot of time to the Requiem, though this was not yet quite ready for the public.

His summer holiday he spent once more in Lichtenthal, so as to be near Clara Schumann. He lingered longer than usual and was still there in October when he received the surprising news that his recently bereaved father was already contemplating another alliance. Undeterred by the unhappy ending of his first matrimonial venture, and anxious to secure a helpmate for his declining years, old Jakob had found a widow, Caroline Schnack, who was willing to become his second wife. She was eighteen years his junior, kept a little restaurant where Jakob went sometimes for a meal and, as Johannes found when he visited his father at the end of the year, was admirably fitted to look after him. The pair were married on 22nd March 1866, and the arrangement turned out an unqualified success. Throughout the business Johannes showed a sympathetic understanding of his father's position that was admirable, realizing the old man's loneliness, appreciating his problem and rejoicing at its solution. His devotion to his dead mother did not prevent him from welcoming Caroline kindly when they met. Indeed the two of them

[1] It is noteworthy that Brahms paid his compliment to Hanslick with the easily apprehended waltzes, and not with a more serious work.

formed a friendship that lasted till Johannes' death; while Fritz Schnack, Caroline's son by her former marriage, became one of the composer's most stalwart admirers.

The loss of his mother drew Brahms closer than ever to his surviving parent, and in August 1867 he persuaded him to come as his guest on a trip to the mountains of Styria, Gänsbacher making a third member of the party. They met in Vienna, and before they left the city Johannes took his father round to meet his friends. During these few days, which would have been trying to a mean nature, he appears at his best, proud of his father and magnificently unconscious of his uncouthness. Vienna rather took to Jakob, who was obviously a 'character,' and was much amused by his treatment of his formidable son. With increasing years and growing fame Johannes' tongue was already developing that sharpness which made him feared as well as admired. On all musical matters Jakob looked up to him with almost comical awe. But in everyday affairs he still treated him much as he had treated him twenty years earlier, laying down the law and meeting any hint of contradiction with a brusque 'Hold your tongue, Hannes!' What is more, 'Hannes' held it. Vienna liked that.

On this tour and on the succeeding one they took to Switzerland in 1868 Johannes was determined that his father should see something of the mountains he had himself come to love on previous visits, and long walks were the order of the day. But the son, in superb health and the full tide of his strength, did not always allow sufficiently for his parent's age. Jakob, who knew only the flat country round the lower Elbe, admired the wild scenery. But the hills were long and steep, the paths rugged, and the pace Johannes set was too much for him. After the 1868 tour he decided regretfully that he could not undertake another. But he was always glad he had gone, he enjoyed impressing his Hamburg cronies with accounts of his mountaineering exploits and he immensely appreciated the long uninterrupted spells he had had of his son's company.

All this while Vienna was steadily tightening her grip on

Brahms. Slowly, imperceptibly, the casual port of call was becoming the base from which all voyages started and to which in the end they all returned. For the voyages continued. Some were holidays, a few were undertaken to visit friends; but the majority of them were concert tours during which Brahms, as conductor or pianist, pursued the double task of earning money and making his music known. He never crossed the sea, and for the most part confined his activities to the German-speaking countries, though he went as far east as Budapest, as far west as Holland and as far north as Denmark. During his early years, when he had been to such a large extent the plaything of circumstance, his life had lacked any regular pattern. Now it began to develop a kind of rhythm. The most usual time for the concert tours was the autumn, and they were designed to bring him back to Vienna for the winter season. But he would often undertake a fresh tour in the spring. In the early summer came his holiday, which he always spent in the country, generally (during the period we are now considering) at Lichtenthal, so that he could visit Clara Schumann, the best of all his friends. It was a long holiday, often extending to several months. He delighted in the country, especially in woods and mountains, as much as his great predecessor, Beethoven. But he was anything but idle. Composition came easiest to him at these periods, to which we owe a considerable proportion of his finest music. The result was that after the 'holiday' he frequently needed a rest; and so we get such tours as those to Styria and Switzerland. After that it was time for the next autumn concert tour.

Naturally his circle of friends increased. Hermann Levi, the conductor, he met at Lichtenthal in the summer of 1864, and Levi did much for the spread of his music till the friendship foundered in 1875 on the ever-dangerous rock of Wagner. A visit to Switzerland in 1865, wherein he combined concert-giving with pleasure, brought two new friends. The first of these, Theodor Billroth, a famous surgeon and an enthusiastic amateur of music, came soon afterwards to live in Vienna; and time and again a new chamber work by Brahms would be tried over for the first time in Billroth's music-room, the host himself taking the viola part. Brahms's friendship with the poet Victor Widmann of Berne, begun during the holidays in Switzerland, ripened more slowly, but became in the end one of the closest of all. Ignaz Brüll, a fine pianist with a phenomenal memory, he had got to know soon after his first arrival in Vienna. Brüll had a profound understanding of his friend's music, and Brahms was always happy when the début of a new work was in his safe and sympathetic hands. In Vienna too he met the poet Max Kalbeck, most faithful of all his followers. Kalbeck ultimately became the author of the standard life of Brahms, a fine, painstaking piece of work, German alike in its length and its thoroughness. Others of the Viennese circle were Gustav Nottebohm, the learned editor of Beethoven's sketch-books, Anton Door, composer and pianist, and C. F. Pohl, registrar of the Vienna Gesellschaft der Musik-freunde (Philharmonic Society). These names are far from exhausting the list, but they must suffice to give some idea of the extent and variety of Brahms's acquaintance.

We may conclude this bird's-eye view of the composer's life during these years of hard work and rising fame with an account of two very different events that both belong to 1868. During the previous year Stockhausen had resigned the conductorship of the Hamburg Philharmonic, and since the committee had once again passed over Brahms when selecting his successor the two friends were free to go off on a concert tour together early that year. All went well at first, and they were particularly gratified by their warm reception in Denmark. The Danes, though still sore after the disastrous Prusso-Danish war, did not allow political prejudice to interfere with music, and after two most successful concerts the visitors from Germany were invited by the Danish composer Niels Gade to meet a representative gathering of Danish musicians. It was at this *soirée* that someone asked Brahms if he had seen the famous Thorwaldsen Museum. 'Yes,' he replied, 'it is quite extraordinary. It is only a pity that it is not in Berlin.'

49

It has been affirmed that *Lilliburlero* sang James II out of England.
This single sentence was even quicker in bundling Brahms out of
Denmark. By the next day it was all over Copenhagen, and so
hot was the indignation at his gratuitous offensiveness that he had
to leave the country immediately, abandoning the rest of the tour.
Stockhausen went on with Joachim, who had providentially
arrived at the critical moment. Brahms returned to Kiel, his
plans in complete disarray, and called on his friend Klaus Groth,
who managed, though not without difficulty, to extract from him
the whole story. Asked by his horrified friend how on earth he
had come to make such an appalling *gaffe* Brahms merely said
that the effect of his remark had not occurred to him. I believe
this to be the simple truth, and I think that here we have the
explanation of many (though not all) of those harsh, rude sayings
that lost him so many friends in later life and established his
reputation as a bear. It was not merely Teutonic lack of sensibility, not merely the coarseness of grain that belonged to his
peasant stock—though he had his full share of both. Brahms
was an introvert. In carrying on a conversation, as in writing
a letter or composing a symphony, his mind looked inward,
focusing itself exclusively on the formulation of his ideas. How
the expression of them might affect another person it seldom
occurred to him to consider.

The Danish episode belongs to March. By 1st April Brahms
was at Bremen, and all memories of unpleasantness at Copenhagen were washed away on 10th April in a flood of triumph
when the German Requiem[1] received its first performance in
Bremen cathedral.

Concerning the origin of this greatest of his choral works it is

---

[1] On this occasion only I yield to convention and call the work the
'German' Requiem. Brahms adopted the title *Deutsches Requiem*
because the words are in German. When the Requiem is sung in
English (as it usually is in this country) the adjective 'German' loses
all meaning. There was no deliberate attempt on Brahms's part to
make his *music* German, and the text is from the Bible.

even more difficult than usual to speak with certainty. Perhaps it had its beginning in the abortive Symphony, written at the time of the Schumann tragedy, which he had already raided for the first movement of the D minor Concerto, and whose slow movement ultimately became the second number of the Requiem.[1] This was next expanded into a cantata of four movements whose text the composer had already arranged in 1861.[2] It is clear therefore that we cannot regard either his mother's death in 1865 or the Austro-Prussian war of 1866 as *fons et origo* of the whole business. The only death that could possibly have inspired its inception was that of Schumann in 1856. But in the absence of definite evidence it seems just as reasonable to regard it merely as the most important of those musings on death that so often occupied Brahms's mind from the *Burial Hymn* of 1858 to the *Four Serious Songs* of 1896. On the other hand, it is quite likely that his mother's death was the impulse that set him to work with renewed energy in 1865 and carried the work to completion in August 1866. By this time it contained six movements and was substantially the Requiem we know, save that the soprano solo had not yet been composed. In 1867 Brahms sent the score to Dietrich, and it was Dietrich who passed it on to Dr. Reinthaler, organist and choirmaster of Bremen cathedral. Reinthaler was eager to secure the work for Bremen, and arrangements were made for its production at the cathedral on Good Friday, 10th April 1868. Meanwhile Herbeck, director of the Vienna Philharmonic concerts, had obtained permission to perform the first three movements in Vienna. This concert took place on 1st December 1867, Herbeck

[1] I reject the theory that a hint from Schumann set Brahms thinking of a German Requiem. Surely it is disposed of by Brahms himself, who wrote to Clara on 22nd December 1888: 'I have just read in an essay by Kalbeck . . . that your husband had made a note of the title *Deutsches Requiem*. This is something quite new to me.'

[2] I follow the account of Dr. Karl Geiringer who, as custodian of the collection of the Vienna *Gesellschaft der Musikfreunde*, has had exceptional opportunities to ascertain the true sequence of events.

himself conducting. But rehearsals had been insufficient and the result was a travesty. In particular the fugue at the end of the third movement was ruined by the misplaced enthusiasm of the drummer, who elected to play the long roll on D that persists throughout the piece at a steady *fortissimo*, effectively swamping the rest of the music.

Reinthaler saw to it that nothing of this sort marred the Bremen performance of the six movements. Nobody had taken the Vienna fiasco too seriously, and as 10th April drew near the attention of all musical Germany was focused on Bremen. Good Friday came, and the cathedral was full to the doors. Joachim was there with his wife (they both contributed to other parts of the programme), as were Max Bruch and Albert Dietrich. Hamburg was well represented: not only had old Jakob come to hear his son's greatest work, but Reinthaler had paid a graceful compliment to Brahms and his native city by including in his chorus some members of the Hamburg Ladies' Choir. Even distant England rendered homage in the person of John Farmer, one of the first and most enthusiastic of the English 'Brahmins.' As he looked round him Johannes had every reason to feel pleased. Just before the music began he had occasion to go to the cathedral door, and there coming up the steps, to his surprise and delight, was Clara Schumann. With a broad smile on his face he led her up the aisle to her seat.

The performance, which Brahms himself conducted, was magnificent. Choir and orchestra had been drilled till they not only knew the work, but loved it. Stockhausen's singing of the baritone solo was inspired. Even Reinthaler was satisfied. As for Brahms, this worthy rendering of his noblest music set the hall-mark upon him. Henceforth he was an accepted master. Nor could the cool reception of the Requiem on 18th February 1869, at Leipzig, when it was performed for the first time with the recently added soprano solo, affect the verdict in any way. The stronghold of the Mendelssohn faction had been the first to reject the D minor Concerto, and others had followed. In failing to appreciate the Requiem it remained alone.

§2. FROM THE REQUIEM TO THE FIRST SYMPHONY (1868–76)

The autograph score of the Requiem was written on sheets of varying size and shape. In later life Brahms was fond of pointing this out to his friends and explaining that when he composed the work he was too poor to buy much paper at a time. We must bear in mind that the copy in question may have dated back to 1866 (and may conceivably have included sheets that Brahms retained unaltered from even earlier labours on the work). If that is so, then the soprano solo would have been inserted in its place later, for it was not completed till May 1868. A score that gradually accumulated in this sort of way would very likely include several varieties of paper. But if the whole copy was made at the same time it cannot be earlier than 1868, and by that time one may doubt whether he was really so short of money as he afterwards pretended. The almost penniless boy who dashed to the rescue of Clara Schumann in 1854 had given place to an artist of established reputation, much in demand as pianist, conductor and teacher, and able to command respectable fees in all three capacities. Moreover, even before the Requiem, his compositions were selling satisfactorily and bringing him money in an increasing stream. Brahms was very lucky in his publisher. It was in 1860 that he met and made friends with Fritz Simrock, of the famous publishing house of that name, and before long Simrock had become his principal publisher. All too often it happens that composer and publisher regard one another as natural enemies. One remembers Beethoven's difficulties, or Dvořák's with this very house of Simrock. But Brahms and Fritz Simrock trusted one another and were thoroughly satisfied with their association. There were even times when Brahms believed, or affected to believe, that Simrock overpaid him, and then he would write quizzing his publisher for his extravagance. The real extent of his confidence he showed in later life when he handed over to Simrock the entire management of his money. Simrock discharged the task faithfully, and Brahms died a rich man.

In 1868 wealth had not yet come to him. One must not forget his manifold expenses on behalf of his family, and his lifelong habit of doing good by stealth, which made inroads upon his purse that no one can estimate. Still, he was not hard pressed. Even before the Requiem Clara in her letters exclaims more than once in surprise at the extent of his resources, while refusing his urgent but rather shamefaced requests that she should take some of his money for herself—as a favour to him. The Requiem made a big difference to his fortunes. He became a famous, even a popular composer, and it was soon possible for him to do as he had always wished and make his writing the main source of his livelihood. He gave up teaching altogether, except when he indulged a whim to instruct some specially gifted student, and he closed his career as a virtuoso pianist. This must not be taken to mean that he ceased to play and even to play in public. He still appeared on the platform, and we hear of him undertaking the tremendous solo part of the B♭ major piano Concerto, which was not introduced to the world till 1881. But after 1869 he no longer devoted much time to his technique. He always remained a fluent, musicianly and most poetic pianist, but the brilliancy, clarity and accuracy that belong only to the virtuoso he was content to forgo.

Soon after the Requiem had brought him fame Brahms began to be lionized—and hated it. The whole tribe of interviewers, autograph-hunters, photographers filled him with disgust and contempt. His reputation for 'bearishness' is largely (though not entirely) due to his efforts to shake off these insects who tormented him and whose persecutions sometimes roused him to an outburst that withered them; for the caustic phrase, the word that wounded sprang to his tongue with fatal ease. One likes to believe that afterwards, in solitude, he regretted the things he said. But there is not much evidence of this, for he never acquired the art of graceful apology. The rare *amendes* wrung from him by an ashamed consciousness of his own injustice were generally halting, semi-articulate affairs that made their recipient almost as uncomfortable as the offence itself.

Between 1867 and 1873 he published scarcely any instrumental music. These are years during which he was preoccupied almost entirely with the voice, and to them belong the greatest pieces of choral music that he ever composed. The supreme masterpiece, the Requiem, was produced, as we have seen, in 1868. It was followed by the dramatic cantata *Rinaldo* and the lovely Alto Rhapsody, both of which were composed in 1869, though the Rhapsody did not get to performance till March of the following year. The *Song of Destiny* was mostly written in 1868, shortly after the Bremen performance of the Requiem. But Brahms was long in finding an ending that satisfied him, and the work was not completed till 1871. The last of these big choral pieces, the *Triumphlied*, commemorated the German victories of 1870 and was composed in the winter of 1870–1, though it did not receive its first performance till 1872. Brahms, who had taken little interest in the Austro-Prussian war of 1866, developed a violent fit of patriotism over the events of 1870, and even considered joining the Prussian forces. He had always disliked the French. But the crisis of the war was over before he could make up his mind, and in the end he wrote the *Triumphlied* instead.

Like the Requiem all these choral works are furnished with orchestral accompaniments, the writing of which brought Brahms fresh ease and confidence in the handling of instruments. So far his only published orchestral compositions had been the D minor piano Concerto and the two Detmold Serenades. All three show traces of inexperience, and perhaps that is why they had no immediate successors. By 1873, however, he felt sufficiently sure of himself to make a new orchestral essay, and in the autumn of that year the Variations on a theme by Haydn were played for the first time at a Vienna concert on 2nd November. In this middle-weight work he handles the instruments like a master, and the Variations may be regarded as a harbinger of the great line of orchestral pieces that begins in 1876 with the first Symphony.

Only a few landmarks merit our attention as the stream of Brahms's life flows gently through these busy years. During the early part of his sojourn in Vienna he had been restless and changed his lodgings frequently. But at the end of 1871 he found rooms that suited him at No. 4 Carlsgasse, and these became his settled home. He had not been there many weeks, however, before bad news sent him in haste to Hamburg, where he arrived in time to take farewell of his father. Old Jakob was suffering from cancer and on 11th February 1872 he died. Johannes' sorrow was deep, but did not prevent his taking practical steps for the welfare of what remained of the family. Caroline, the widow, refused to lay an unnecessary burden on her generous stepson and returned to her former occupation of a boarding-house keeper. Her son, Fritz Schnack, Johannes established in business as a clockmaker at Pinneburg, and he made it possible for Caroline to join him there when the time came for her to retire. Fritz Brahms had been somewhat estranged from his brother for several years. He was a musician, and Johannes' success made him jealous. The nickname of 'the wrong Brahms' bestowed on him by the Hamburgers cannot have been easy to bear and wins him our sympathy. At their father's death-bed the two were reconciled, though they never drew closely together. Fritz died in 1886. Elise, the sister, married in 1871 a watchmaker named Grund, an alliance that caused Johannes some anxiety at first, but turned out much better than any one had expected. He made her a liberal annuity which continued till her death in 1892.

A few months after his father's death Brahms was invited to become conductor of the Vienna Philharmonic Society. His long hesitation was probably due to the familiar internal struggle between love of a fixed post and anxiety for his independence, but in the end he accepted and was in charge of the society's concerts for three years. The Philharmonic was a flourishing, entirely healthy organization, very different from the limping Academy of Singing he had conducted eight years previously. Its chorus was three hundred strong and its orchestra, already numerous, was brought by the new conductor up to a hundred players. Vienna was by now thoroughly Brahms-conscious and anxious

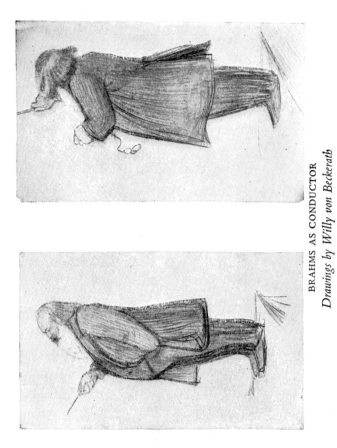

BRAHMS AS CONDUCTOR
*Drawings by Willy von Beckerath*

to hear his music, so that in the course of the three seasons he was able to produce all his big choral works from the Requiem to the *Triumphlied*, some of them twice, as well as the Haydn Variations. Compositions by contemporary or recently dead composers included works by Schumann, Berlioz's *Harold in Italy* and Joachim's Hungarian Concerto. The classics were represented by such masterpieces as Handel's Dettingen *Te Deum*, Bach's St. Matthew Passion and the Beethoven Mass in D, and Brahms did not fail to give his audiences some examples of the sixteenth-century *a cappella* music he loved so well. His thorough understanding of old music was particularly valuable. Dr. Geiringer, who is in a position to know, says that Vienna owes much to Brahms's scholarship, particularly as regards works of the seventeenth and early eighteenth centuries. He set his face against the reorchestration of the old scores and reinstated the *continuo* in its proper position. These Philharmonic concerts are also remarkable in that they provided the only occasion when Brahms and Bruckner ever appeared on the same platform. Brahms's very strong prejudice against Bruckner had no personal basis and was mostly due to Bruckner's unqualified Wagnerism. This warped his judgment and made him a good deal less than just to his contemporary.

The last of the Philharmonic concerts that Brahms conducted took place on 18th April 1875, the solo singer on this occasion being Georg Henschel. Brahms first met Henschel, who was a native of Breslau, in 1874, and the two quickly formed a firm friendship. In 1876 they spent a holiday together on the island of Rügen, in the Baltic. Henschel, who became a British subject in 1890, outlived Brahms, and survived (as Sir George Henschel) to carry the great traditions of German *Lieder*-singing into a later generation, besides supplying us with many interesting sidelights on the great man who had been his friend. It was Henschel too who introduced the young Ethel Smyth to Brahms. She became a pupil of Heinrich von Herzogenberg and met Johannes at the Herzogenberg house. But that was at a rather later date.

When Brahms resigned the directorship of the Philharmonic Society in 1875 he was closing his career as an 'all purposes' conductor. Never again was he to accept a permanent or semi-permanent position of this sort. He conducted, to be sure, many a time and oft in the years that were to follow, and in many places; but he confined his appearances to occasions when he could introduce and interpret his own orchestral music. Other men, less preoccupied with composition, were, he felt, better able to afford the time for study and rehearsal without which the masterpieces of his predecessors and contemporaries could not be adequately presented. Himself, he had other work to do.

## §3. THE SYMPHONIST (1876–87)

Every student of Brahms has noticed that he produced no string quartet till the C minor (Op. 51, No. 1), finished at Tutzing in 1873, his forty-first year; and no symphony till the work in the same key (Op. 68), completed at Lichtenthal during the autumn of 1876 and first performed at Karlsruhe on 4th November of the same year. Remembering his veneration for Beethoven and that composer's supreme achievements in the domain of quartet and symphony, we have little difficulty in guessing whose hand held the flaming sword that kept him so long from the threshold. He was well aware that one day he must cross it, but he was not going to do so till he felt fully prepared for the ordeal of facing Beethoven on Beethoven's chosen ground. He was always cautious. Perhaps in this case he was over-cautious. Perhaps he delayed too long.

Of course he knew perfectly well what Vienna was thinking. The Viennese had decided that he was Beethoven's heir and in that faith were awaiting his first Symphony with bated breath. When it came[1] it seemed at first to contain the justification of their hopes. Its very key suggests the most famous of Beethoven's

[1] The first Vienna performance was at a Philharmonic concert on 17th December 1876.

symphonies; its first movement is of all Brahms's symphonic movements the most akin to Beethoven in its grim, heroic striving; and the theme of its finale has a passing reminiscence of the finale to Beethoven's ninth Symphony which, as the composer said, 'any donkey can see.' What wonder that enthusiasts talked of 'the tenth symphony,' when even the cool-headed Hanslick could write: 'No other composer has come so near to the magnificent creations of Beethoven as Brahms in the close of the C minor Symphony'?

But it would be hard to recall a single instance of the mature Brahms allowing his judgment as a composer to be influenced by public clamour. The verdict of a Marxsen, a Joachim, an Elisabeth von Herzogenberg he sought and respected, but for the opinion of the mob he entertained only a healthy contempt. Nor had he any illusions as to the modesty of his own stature as compared with Beethoven's. 'Do you know,' he once said scornfully to Josef Labor, 'there are asses in Vienna who take me for a second Beethoven?'[1] If he hesitated to produce a symphony it was not Vienna's judgment that he feared but the inexorable verdict of his own artistic integrity. This was holy ground, sanctified by Beethoven's incomparable achievements. If Brahms was to approach it he must do so humbly; no offering would be worthy that fell short of the utmost that was in him.

The intense self-criticism that made him build bonfires of his compositions as a boy and destroy works on which even Schumann had set the seal of his approval, is thus seen functioning at its most implacable when he is following in Beethoven's footsteps. The Quartet in C minor was not the first he wrote, nor the second; it was only the first he allowed to survive. In the same way (so Sir Donald Tovey has told us) the violin Sonata in G, Op. 78, known to us as his first, was actually his fifth. It is impossible to say how many symphonies Brahms composed before the C minor. We know of one, the work he used as a quarry for the first piano Concerto and the Requiem. If we cannot be sure that there were

[1] I have this story from Mr. Paul Wittgenstein.

more, that is because the C minor itself has its roots so deep in the past. Its first movement, at any rate, goes back to the dark years of Schumann's illness. By 1862 it was well advanced, for Clara Schumann and Dietrich had both seen it. In the Requiem year (1868) Brahms was thinking of the finale, as we know from his letter to Clara of 12th September. 'Thus blew the shepherd's horn to-day,' he exclaims, and follows the words with a stave of music:

But whatever the sources of its inspiration the Symphony, as we now have it, is the work of a completely mature Brahms. Perhaps it was in 1874 that he set to work seriously giving it its definitive form. Its completion in 1876 may mark the end of a process that had taken twenty years.

Cambridge was the first English centre to hear the Symphony. The enthusiasm of that ardent Brahms-admirer, Charles Villiers Stanford, then at the outset of his distinguished career, induced the faculty of music at the University to offer Brahms an honorary doctorate. Since the degree could not be conferred *in absentia* it was necessary for Brahms to come to Cambridge to get it; and that, of course, was what Stanford wanted. Almost the plan succeeded. Brahms was flattered. He agreed to come — and then at the last moment changed his mind. He hated the sea, and it may have been the Channel crossing that deterred him; or perhaps it was a not altogether groundless fear that a fuss would be made of him. But Joachim, who had also been offered a doctorate and had accepted, was entrusted by Brahms with the manuscript of the Symphony in acknowledgment of the compliment; and he conducted the work at a concert on 8th March 1877, together with the *Song of Destiny* and his own *Tragic Overture*.[1]

The big landmarks of the next two years are both orchestral. Having taken twenty years over his first Symphony Brahms produced his second little more than a year later, and it received its first performance in Vienna on 30th December 1877, under Hans Richter. Most of the work had been done in the course of a summer 'holiday' at Pörtschach in Carinthia. Pörtschach seems to have suited Brahms, for it was there in the following year that he wrote most of the violin Concerto for which Joachim had so long been asking him. It was produced at Leipzig on 1st January 1879, Brahms conducting and Joachim, to whom it was dedicated, playing the solo part. A third summer at Pörtschach saw the birth of the less imposing but scarcely less beautiful violin Sonata in G.

In March 1879 Breslau University, following the example of Cambridge, offered Brahms an honorary doctorate. He sent a postcard to his Breslau friend, Bernhard Scholz, asking him to acknowledge the honour on his behalf, and apparently thought he had done all that was required of him. Scholz quickly disillusioned him: he must write a new symphony for the occasion, or at least 'a festive song.' For the summer of 1880 he tried a new holiday resort, Ischl in the Salzkammergut,[2] and there he settled down to produce something for Breslau. The certificate conferring the doctorate referred to him as 'viro illustrissimo ... artis musicae severioris in Germania nunc principi.' Perhaps, as one of his

---

[1] For a fuller account of this incident see H. Plunket Greene's *Charles Villiers Stanford*.

[2] Ischl was a success. He returned there in 1882, and from 1889 to the end of his life he visited it every year. It was not far from Vienna, a consideration that weighed with him increasingly as he grew older, and it was a favourite resort of Hanslick, Johann Strauss and other friends.

biographers suggests, the word 'severioris' woke a spirit of mischief in him. The *Academic Festival Overture* is based on four student songs and their treatment is much more festive than academic. The orchestra is the largest Brahms ever employed, and the work ends with an uproarious version of 'Gaudeamus igitur,' which made its due effect on the students when the overture received its first performance at Breslau on 4th January 1881, the new doctor himself conducting. Feeling perhaps that the piece occupied a rather solitary place among his compositions, Brahms gave it a companion, working up some sketches that probably belong to the late 1860s[1] into the *Tragic Overture*. This was also completed at Ischl in the summer of 1880, and performed for the first time in Vienna on 20th December.

For the summer of 1881 Brahms established himself at Press-baum, near Vienna. Here he finished the huge piano Concerto in B♭ major, on which he had started working in 1878. This year also brought a revival of interest in large-scale choral music. His setting of Schiller's *Nänie* was finished, like the Concerto, at Pressbaum and dedicated to the memory of his friend Anselm Feuerbach, the painter. It was followed in 1882 by Goethe's gloomy *Song of the Fates*, for which the music was composed during the summer at Ischl. But these were digressions from the main stream of his thought, which was still orchestral. In 1883 he finished the third Symphony, which Richter con-ducted at its first performance (Vienna, 2nd December); and in 1884 he was already busy with the fourth, though this took rather longer and was not introduced to the public till 25th October 1885 at a concert at Meiningen. After it there came a pause. Brahms's one remaining orchestral work, the double Concerto for violin and cello, was not composed till the summer of 1887. This year his 'holiday' was at Thun, in Switzerland, and one commentator suggests that the magnificent mountain scenery may have found a reflection in the music of the Concerto.[2] The

[1] See Geiringer: *Brahms: his Life and Work.*
[2] See De Beer: *Escape to Switzerland.*

first performance was at Cologne on 15th October 1887. The composer conducted, Joachim and Hausmann were the soloists.

Against this background of imposing masterpieces the every-day happenings of a laborious, uneventful life inevitably wear a somewhat trivial aspect. Brahms composed, he went on concert tours in the interests of his music, he took his holidays where his fancy led him. Billroth had long been urging him to visit Italy, and in 1878 he gained his point. Brahms and Goldmark, with Billroth as their *cicerone,* set out together in April. They saw Florence, Rome and Venice, and went as far south as Naples. At once and irretrievably Brahms fell under the spell of Italian scenery and Italian architecture (though never of Italian music), and it drew him south again and again. He went eight times in all to Italy, Widmann being his chosen companion on the later journeys.

In September 1878 he was in Hamburg, conducting his second Symphony. The occasion is notable for two reasons: first, it marked his reconciliation with the town of his birth; the sense of injury engendered by the Philharmonic's rejection of him in 1862 and 1867 was obliterated at long last by the enthusiastic reception of the Symphony and buried under the shower of roses that fell upon him from all sides at the work's conclusion. Secondly, it was at this concert that his great beard made its first public appearance, to the surprise of all his admirers and the consternation of some. A previous experiment with it had been abandoned after a brief trial. But he had grown it again in Italy, and now it became a permanency.

To keep track of the constant changes in his wide circle of friends is beyond our scope. We must content ourselves with a glance at two of the most striking personalities that influenced him in these years of achievement. Elisabeth von Stockhausen[1] was born in Paris in 1847, the daughter of a diplomat. In due course she became a pupil of Epstein in Vienna. She was beautiful, she was intelligent, she was most musical. She could sing as well as play the piano, she had an astonishingly quick ear

[1] She was not related to Julius Stockhausen, the singer.

that enabled her to pick up the most complex progression at a single hearing, and a retentive memory. It is surprising to find Epstein handing over such a paragon to Brahms soon after the latter's arrival in Vienna, and even more surprising that Brahms should have sent her back to Epstein after a few lessons. Perhaps there is something in the story that both teachers were a little afraid of her and got rid of her for their own peace of mind. She reappears in Brahms's life in 1874 as Elisabeth von Herzogenberg. Heinrich von Herzogenberg, himself a professional musician and an ardent admirer of Brahms, was then living at Leipzig, and it was mainly due to his efforts and his wife's that Leipzig adventured on a 'Brahms week' at the end of January. The composer came. He played and conducted with notable success. Every one was pleased; the Mendelssohn fortress capitulated; Johannes found himself with two new friends.

The volume containing the correspondence between them[1] is one that no Brahms-lover should miss, for it shows better than anything else the lovable side of his nature. The old bear could unbend, he could even dance when Elisabeth piped the tune. Her letters, all sunshine and quicksilver, are none the less full of shrewd criticism. She can praise generously and wisely, but she has no hesitation about drawing his attention to passages in his works that she finds dubious, and often she persuades him to alter them. She is not in the least afraid of him, this 'slender woman in blue velvet with golden hair,' and she rates him soundly at the least sign of crustiness. Her husband, a learned but pedestrian composer, would sometimes submit a work of his own for Brahms's criticism. That always meant a bad moment for Johannes. He was incapable of a dishonest judgment on any musical matter, and we watch him ponderously manœuvring to avoid expressing any opinion at all. But Elisabeth is inexorable, and in the end he has to say what he thinks, one eye on his artistic integrity, the other, a very apprehensive eye, on the wrath to come.

[1] *Johannes Brahms: the Herzogenberg Correspondence*, edited by Max Kalbeck and translated by Hannah Bryant.

And come it does, for Elisabeth can be an avenging angel in her husband's interest, even when it is a Brahms who dares to give him less than she considers his due. A long illness of Heinrich's in 1888 and the removal of the Herzogenbergs to distant Berlin had the effect of loosening the tie between them and Brahms. But it never snapped, and Elisabeth's death in 1892 was a profound grief to the composer. For long her photograph had stood in his room; and there it remained, almost to the end.

If Brahms's orchestral works won universal acceptance throughout Germany during their composer's lifetime much of the credit must go to their greatest interpreter, Hans von Bülow. Bülow had been a shining light in the neo-German school and Wagner's closest associate in Munich. It is easy to regard the transference of his allegiance to Brahms as the result of pique, and indeed it would be very extraordinary if pique had not played its part, for Bülow had married Cosima, Liszt's daughter, and she had forsaken him for Wagner; so that Bülow's departure from the Liszt-Wagner camp was not so much a deliberate secession as a violent ejection. The poor man was thrown upon the world without a wife, almost without a friend; and by a cruel stroke of fate he was even debarred from the pursuit of his main object in life, the furtherance of Wagner's musical ideals. But even so he was far too deep and sincere a musician to attach himself to Brahms merely to spite Wagner. At first perhaps he had nothing to cling to amid the ruin of his hopes but his veneration for Beethoven, whose works he interpreted with an insight that Wagner alone could rival. It was only gradually that he came to see how the Beethoven tradition which Wagner had (in his own phrase) 'diverted into the channel of the musical drama' might also be made to flow in the symphonic bed that Brahms provided. Not till the appearance of the first Symphony was Bülow's conversion completed. But once convinced he put all the energy, all the talents, all the selfless devotion he had lavished on Wagner at the service of Johannes, finding in him a new purpose for his desolate existence. In 1880 he was appointed musical director to the

Duke of Saxe-Meiningen. The orchestra was small, a mere fifty all told, but with the active support of the duke, whose enthusiasm for music in general and Brahms in particular was only second to Bülow's own, he raised it to a pitch of excellence that brought it a reputation out of all proportion to its size; and he used it as a sort of crusading army on his friend's behalf, travelling with it far and wide throughout Germany. The B♭ major Concerto and the fourth Symphony are perhaps the works for which Bülow did most, and it was another of the ironies of fate that this Symphony should have been the cause of a quarrel with Brahms and the resignation of his Meiningen position late in 1885. A clumsy letter of Brahms's was at the root of the trouble, which lasted two years. Then, in 1887, Bülow, who was a superb pianist as well as a conductor of genius, visited Vienna to play the complete cycle of Beethoven's sonatas. From the audience at one of the concerts Brahms sent him a card on which he had written the music only of the phrase to which Pamina (in *The Magic Flute*) sings 'Shall I then see thee nevermore?' It was as near an apology as he could get. Reconciliation followed, and Bülow remained faithful till his death in 1894.

But for a man well advanced in middle age the account of friendship has two sides. Nottebohm died in 1882; in 1887 Pohl and Marxsen passed away. More grievous still to Johannes was the loss, but not through death, of the oldest of all his friends, the trusty Joachim. For several years they had been drifting apart. To some extent it was the fault of circumstances that limited their opportunities of seeing one another. But that was not all. The perfect sympathy that united them in youth did not survive in its entirety the passage of the years. As early as 1867 we find Joachim criticizing Brahms in a letter to Amalie, and the next year Brahms and Clara Schumann are shaking their heads over what they regard as Joachim's worldliness. But despite this and other jars they managed to keep the barque of friendship afloat till in 1881 it was finally wrecked on the rock of Joachim's matrimonial troubles.

Joachim's character, in many ways so admirable, had a serious flaw: he was madly and quite unreasonably jealous of his wife. Jealousy imposes a strain against which no marriage bond can hold indefinitely, and by 1880 Brahms was so concerned about their evident estrangement that he ventured to exercise the privilege of an old friend and lecture them both, not concealing from 'Jussuf' that he considered him chiefly to blame. Next year Joachim sought him out at Pressbaum and they had a further discussion. Again Brahms took Amalie's side, and again he failed to convince his friend. The argument probably waxed hot, and under its influence Johannes wrote to Amalie, saying some sharp things about her husband and vouching for her innocence on the charge of adultery that Joachim had levelled against her—though how Brahms could know anything definite of so intimate a matter is obscure. Amalie replied, asking whether she might make use of this letter, and Johannes most imprudently gave the required permission. Probably he had forgotten how intemperately he had written, certainly he did not foresee the consequences. His dismay may be imagined when Joachim sued for divorce and this very letter was produced in court for the defence. Coming as it did from Joachim's oldest friend it carried great weight and in the end decided the case against him. Joachim was cut to the heart, and he cannot be blamed for breaking off all relations with this 'faithless friend.'

For a while the breach was absolute, though Joachim demonstrated his artistic integrity by continuing to work as before on behalf of Brahms's music. Brahms certainly felt uncomfortable about the results of his indiscretion, and in the course of the next few years he made more than one gesture towards the great artist he had so grievously offended. Eventually, in 1887, he succeeded in patching up the quarrel by means of the double Concerto, and after that the two often met without apparent embarrassment, though never again without restraint. The artistic partnership was resumed, but the old intimacy had vanished.

In this same year Brahms received the Prussian order *Pour le mérite*. It was a high distinction and he valued it the more that his name appeared in company with Treitschke, Gustav Freytag and Verdi. But did he feel a pang at the thought that no longer could he take his good news and pour it into the ear of a sympathetic 'Jussuf'?

Wm. Pithan

Berlin W. 30

Breitkopf & Härtel

# CHAPTER IV

## CADENCE

### §1. Indian Summer (1887–96)

FLORENCE MAY gives an account of Brahms as she saw him in Vienna in 1888. 'He looked an old man,' she says. 'His hair was nearly white, and he had grown very stout.' But if he could no longer outwalk his friends on a mountain path there were compensations. 'He now wore the happy, sunshiny look of one who had realized his purpose and was content with his share in life.' Unremitting labour consistently devoted to a single object had brought him first mastery, then universal acknowledgment. He could afford now to relax a little and savour the fruits of success. Of these the one that pleased him most was the honorary freedom conferred on him by Hamburg in 1889. How often and how vainly he had wooed Hamburg in earlier years! Now, it seemed, she came to him of her own accord—though Bülow, now living in Hamburg, could have told a story of patient diplomacy lying behind the apparently spontaneous gesture. Brahms came in September for the formal handing over of the documents, and the Hamburg Cecilia Society made this the occasion for a five-days' festival, at which were performed (among other things) the three *Fest- und Gedenksprüche* in eight parts, which the composer had written for the occasion and dedicated to the burgomaster. In 1894 he was offered the conductorship of the Philharmonic concerts. 'There are not many things I so long and fervently desired at one time,' he says in his reply. But now it was too late. Brahms and Hamburg had said their farewells in 1889, though neither was aware of it; and they parted friends.

His health remained excellent. But after 1889 there is a noticeable abatement of his physical activity, for which his increasing corpulence may have been partly responsible. He felt disinclined now to undertake arduous concert tours, for which indeed there was no longer any necessity; and from 1889 onwards he spent all his summers at Ischl among his friends and within reach of Vienna. Only the hankering for Italy remained, drawing him south in 1890 and again in 1893. Vienna had plans for celebrating his sixtieth birthday, and it was partly his dislike of a fuss that determined him on this 1893 tour. In the course of their wanderings his companion, Widmann, hurt his foot, and Brahms spent his birthday sitting quietly at his friend's bedside.

The spate of compositions dwindles considerably during these last years. But there is no falling off in quality, and the string Quintet in G major, completed in 1890, is among the freshest and most spontaneous of his works. He had a mind to make this the last of all his creations, to lay down his pen for ever; and perhaps he might have done so if he had not happened in 1891 to pay a visit to the castle at Meiningen, where he was always a welcome and honoured guest. Here his attention was attracted by the superb playing of Richard Mühlfeld, clarinettist in the duke's orchestra. He was so impressed by the possibilities of the clarinet revealed to him by Mühlfeld's performances that when he got to Ischl in the summer he settled down to write two chamber works, a Trio and a Quintet, with a part for the clarinet. In 1894 he further enriched the clarinet repertory with the two Sonatas in F minor and E♭ major. Mühlfeld's performance of these pieces was a source of never-ending delight to Brahms, who took a sincere liking to the clarinettist, introducing him to all his friends as 'my prima donna.'

Neither the clarinet Trio nor the Sonatas will stand comparison with the splendid Quintet. But over all four works there shines a benign, mellow light not to be found in his earlier compositions. We meet it again in the sheaf of pieces, Opp. 116, 117, 118 and 119, with which he closed the list of his piano works. It may be, as Fuller Maitland believed, that these trifles are not all the product of a single fit of creative activity, but had been gradually accumulating ever since the two Rhapsodies of 1880. But the sensitive listener will, I think, feel fairly confident that a considerable number of them belong to this ripest phase of Brahms's maturity. They have that flavour. The same cannot be said of the forty-nine *Deutsche Volkslieder*, published in 1894. These are arrangements, not original compositions, and they represent a lifetime's gleanings. At the very end of them he placed 'Verstohlen geht der Mond auf,' the tune on which he had based the variations of his piano Sonata, Op. 1. 'The snake bites its own tail,' he said,[1] a clear indication that with the *Volkslieder* he meant to round off his life's work. There were, however, still two postscripts to come, the *Vier ernste Gesänge* of 1896 and the Eleven Chorale Preludes for organ (completed in the same year and published posthumously).

Tokens frequently reached him of the esteem in which he was held by many, though not all, of his fellow composers. Dvořák, of course, was deeply in his debt. In 1876, when the Czech composer was still struggling in obscurity, Brahms and Hanslick, as members of a government committee, obtained for him a grant of money that not only contributed to the relief of his necessities, but provided him with much-wanted encouragement, and Brahms had followed this up by giving him an enthusiastic introduction to his own publisher, Simrock. Nor did his kindness stop there, and Dvořák owed more of his success to Brahms than to any one. His gratitude was eager and generous. Brahms on his side had a genuine admiration for Dvořák's music, and tried hard to persuade him to settle in Vienna. In this he was unsuccessful. But Dvořák visited Vienna several times and never failed to pay his respects to his benefactor. The last occasion was in February 1896, when the two composers sat together in a box listening to the first performance in Vienna of the 'New World' Symphony.

Grieg was another composer who interested Brahms, the Norwegian's effective use of the folksongs of his own country winning the German's cordial approval. They met for the last time when

[1] It is Specht who has preserved this remark.

Grieg was in Vienna in March 1896, and as soon as he got back home Grieg wrote a charming letter inviting Brahms to Norway, where (says Grieg) he will surely find the inspiration for his fifth Symphony. With Mahler too Brahms was on friendly terms, though inclined to shake his head over Mahler's music. It must be admitted that his sympathy was hard to engage for music whose aims and methods differed markedly from his own. The very intensity with which he perceived his own ideal put his vision out of focus when he had to judge music of an altogether different kind. From Wagner he could not withhold a reluctant admiration. But he never abated his hostility to Liszt and Bruckner, he was indifferent to Rubinstein and Tchaikovsky and insensitive to the genius of Verdi. The musical trends that were showing themselves in Vienna towards the end of his life he regarded with disapproval. Richard Strauss did not interest him; Hugo Wolf was his declared enemy (though that, to be sure, was altogether Wolf's fault). In general we may say that the young composer who submitted his work to Brahms's criticism took his courage in both hands. Josef Suk once appeared before the master with a Quartet that was to be dedicated to him. Brahms received him kindly and answered his modest protestations with 'If a young man brings me the best thing he can possibly make, such a gift must be accepted with thanks. Of course you can bring no Beethoven C minor Symphony to dedicate to me.' A pause followed—then: 'Nor can I to you.' He began to turn over the pages and complained that there were too many notes. 'The essential thing is that every note should be in its place. I can't do that—nor can Dvořák—and you, of course, least of all.' Suk went out feeling he had been patted with one hand and had his ears boxed with the other.[1]

One new friendship remains to be chronicled. All his life Brahms was susceptible to the charms of a beautiful voice, especially a contralto voice. Alice Barbi not only possessed a

[1] I transcribe this anecdote almost word for word as I had it from Mr. Paul Wittgenstein. He was told it by Suk himself.

rich contralto but used it with admirable artistry. They met in 1890. The man who had escaped unwed from the many senti-mental entanglements of his youth was not likely to make a fool of himself in late middle age, and in spite of at least one bio-grapher's conviction to the contrary it is improbable that the innocent flirtation between Alice and Johannes concealed any-thing more inflammable than a sincere friendship. But he had a profound admiration for her singing and so deep a confidence in her taste that when she sang his songs he even permitted her to meddle with the text. 'Alter it as you like,' he said to her. In 1893 Alice got engaged to be married, and on 21st December she gave her farewell concert. Brahms figured on the programme only as composer, but at the last moment he marched on to the platform and accompanied her throughout.[1]

No. 4 Carlsgasse was still his home.[2] His rooms were not very conveniently arranged, but he had grown used to them, and he would not have dreamed of parting with his landlady, Frau Truxa, who understood him as well as any one. She had two children, and when she was away on her lawful occasions Brahms never failed to look in twice a day so as to be sure the little ones were properly cared for; nor would he permit the maid to do his own rooms, bidding her devote the time to the children. Hearing of this from the maid Frau Truxa on her return attempted to thank her lodger. Immediately he became inaccessible. Grati-tude embarrassed him. But he was happy when the children called him 'Onkel Bahms.'

Here in these rooms he spent much of his time, working, reading, thinking, playing the piano, perhaps showing his friends some

---

[1] This was only one of many such kindly actions. One recalls, for instance, his goodness to little Marie Soldat, the violinist, a few years earlier. Impressed by her playing he went to great pains to bring her to the notice of Joachim, and continued afterwards to further her career with a fine combination of tact and goodwill.

[2] No. 4 Carlsgasse is still intact after the war.

of the treasures from the fine collection in his library. But he kept to his walks in the city or the Prater, and in these later days was far more ready than formerly to lunch or dine at a friend's house, where he appreciated good cooking and a sound vintage. If no invitation was forthcoming he would betake himself to one of the many restaurants or taverns where he was well known. The more pretentious establishments saw little of him, and his favourite resort was the unassuming but comfortable 'Red Hedgehog.' Even here he would avoid the main dining-room, where he might be stared at by the curious, preferring the little room at the back, intended for a humbler grade of patron, where he could eat at ease in the company, perhaps, of a crony or two.

His sister and Elisabeth von Herzogenberg both died in 1892, and in 1894 Bülow's sad life came to an end. Of his more distant friends only Clara Schumann and Widmann continued to occupy much of his time now that he had ceased to travel much, and he became more and more bound up with the Viennese circle. But in this too time was making ominous gaps. Spitta, the biographer of Bach, and Billroth both died in 1894. With his friends falling all around him Johannes would not fail to ask himself the inevitable question: 'When will my turn come?'

## §2. ILLNESS AND DEATH (1896–7)

In January 1896 Brahms was in Berlin. He conducted his two piano Concertos which d'Albert played, and attended a dinner given by Joachim. The violinist proposed the toast of 'the most famous composer,' but Brahms, seeing what was coming, interposed hastily with: 'Quite right: here's to Mozart!' and clinked glasses all round. It was a cheerful evening, and no one dreamt that the hero of it had just conducted for the very last time.

He spent the spring in Vienna, where, as we have seen, he received visits from Dvořák and Grieg. But an anxious time began towards the end of March. On the 26th Clara Schumann, who had been living for many years at Frankfort, had a slight stroke. She rallied, and throughout April the news was good. But the illness of his oldest and dearest friend certainly affected Brahms and may have had its share in giving his thoughts the grave turn that led to the composition of the *Four Serious Songs*. These he wrote at the end of April or the beginning of May, and they were intended, so he said, as a birthday present to himself. When the day (7th May) came round he was delighted to get a line from Clara, written in bed: 'Heartiest good wishes from your affectionate and devoted Clara Schumann. I cannot do any more yet, but or soon your . . .' The feeble scrawl lapses into illegibility. Much relieved, and believing the danger at an end, Brahms left Vienna for Ischl.

Not many days later the blow fell. Clara had another stroke, and on 20th May she died. Brahms set off at once on the long, trying, cross-country journey that would bring him to the funeral. During the night he had to change at Linz and he arranged with one of the train officials to wake him. But the man forgot and he missed his connection. There was nothing for it but to take a slow train. When at last he reached Frankfort it was to find that the service was over and that Clara had been taken to Bonn to be laid beside her husband. On therefore to Bonn! After thirty-six hours of arduous travel he arrived at the graveside, hot, weary and dishevelled, and was in time to cast his handful of earth on the coffin of the lady he had loved most of all. But the strain, coming immediately on the shock of his bereavement, had shaken him badly. He caught a chill, and it was some days before he could undertake the return journey to Ischl. Established once more in his lodgings he resumed his normal life, working at the Chorale Preludes for organ, all eleven of which he probably finished by the end of June, going for walks and following his usual social routine. But his friends were concerned to notice a change in his appearance. His face lost its customary tan and became increasingly yellow as the weeks wore on. He made no complaint, and for some while no one ventured to tackle him about his health, for his hatred of sickness and the pride he took in his constitution were well known. But the symptoms grew more and more marked, and at last in July Richard Heuberger, the composer, who was organist at Ischl, took his courage in both hands and urged him to see a doctor. It looks as if Brahms himself was secretly anxious, for he received the kindly advice with unexpected mildness and acted on it at once. He was told he had a mild attack of jaundice, and this diagnosis was presently confirmed by Professor Leopold von Schrötter, a Vienna specialist who happened to be at Ischl. He had better go to Carlsbad and take the waters. To Heuberger, however, the doctors told a very different story. Brahms's condition was serious. The bile-ducts were completely closed and there were ominous swellings in the liver. Von Schrötter indeed went further and pronounced him doomed. 'Poor fellow,' he said with reference to the Carlsbad visit, 'it does not matter where he spends his money.'

Brahms liked Carlsbad, but it did him no good and on 2nd October he was back in Vienna. There he was examined by his own doctor. Hitherto there had been some doubt whether he was suffering from cirrhosis or cancer. Now the diagnosis was definite. Brahms had cancer, like his father before him, and the infection had spread to his liver.[1] Of this, however, he was told nothing, and he continued to lead his ordinary life so far as his increasing weakness would permit, lunching and dining out with his friends and frequenting the 'Red Hedgehog' as before. But Richard Specht, who saw much of him at this time, describes his horror at his appearance. Brahms was rapidly losing weight. His face, which retained its jaundiced appearance, had become almost gaunt. His strength was failing and he grew easily tired.

What, one may ask, did he himself really think? Brahms was no fool. Surely there can be little doubt that as the year drew to its close (if not before) he knew that his sickness was mortal and was facing death in his own way. He hated illness and he hated

[1] This was confirmed at the post-mortem.

fuss. Above all he was determined to become a burden to nobody, to be indebted to nobody. And so, as far as he might, he behaved as though nothing were the matter, discouraged all references to his health and begged his doctor 'to tell him nothing unpleasant.' Death he feared, for he had no belief in the here-after, and the prospect of sheer annihilation must daunt even the stoutest heart. This may have been one of the reasons for his assumption of an optimism with which he could mislead his friends and perhaps, sometimes, deceive himself. Thus Joachim, who saw him in December, could write to Grimm that his illness was not so serious and there were good hopes of his recovery. As time went on he became too weak to take his customary walks. But the Fabers, the Fellingers and others came to the rescue with their carriages. He could drive whenever he liked, he could still visit his friends. Inevitably, however, he was much alone. During the last weeks of 1896 he spent many hours tearing up old letters and unpublished manuscripts. He was determined to fore-stall, as far as he could, the indiscretion of biographers and to leave no music unworthy of his own high standard to the mercy of enterprising publishers. Often too he sat at the piano playing or improvising, or in his arm-chair reading. When fatigue overcame him he would close the piano, put down the book and abandon himself to his thoughts, recalling his triumphs, regretting (as all must do) his failures and sometimes, it may be, wrestling with an angel.

Not always could he maintain the optimistic pose. Hausmann, the cellist, came to see him, and together they played Dvořák's cello Concerto. Brahms was enraptured. 'Had I known that such a cello concerto as that could be written I would have tried to compose one myself.' 'Would have!' He knew that the time for such things was over. Round Christmas he was at the Fellingers' and proposed a toast 'to our meeting in the New Year!' Then he became thoughtful and presently muttered, pointing downwards: 'But I shall soon be there.'[1]

[1] Florence May tells this story.

So long as he could he took part in the social and musical life of Vienna. He was present at two concerts by the Joachim Quartet on 1st and 2nd January 1897. At the second they played his G major Quintet, and he acknowledged the applause with tears in his eyes. On 7th March he attended a Philharmonic concert at which Richter conducted the E minor Symphony. The audience became aware of his presence and at the end they rose at him, hands clapping, handkerchiefs fluttering. From a box the shrunken, pain-racked figure acknowledged this last and greatest of his ovations. He was very anxious to hear Johann Strauss's operetta *Die Göttin der Vernunft* on 13th March, but his strength was not equal to it, and he had to leave before the end. The last time he heard chamber music was less than a fortnight before his death, when he dragged himself to the house of another old friend, Frau Wittgenstein, where the Joachim Quartet and Mühlfeld were assembled. Two clarinet quintets were to be rehearsed, his own and Weber's. But Brahms was too weak to sit through both, and they asked him which he would prefer to hear. He chose the Weber.[1]

Even after he had taken to his bed on 26th March he preserved the fiction of his recovery, writing to his stepmother at Pinneburg that as his illness is proving obstinate he is trying what a spell in bed will do. She is not to be anxious. But the end was close now. Dr. Breuer, his medical attendant at this time, had no illusions about his condition and one object only, to spare him pain. March turned to April and on the night of the 2nd he was visibly dying. Frau Truxa watched over him with Dr. Breuer's son, who was also in the medical profession. 'Ah,' said Brahms, when Breuer gave him a glass of hock, 'that tastes good, thank you.'[2] Towards morning Frau Truxa left the room for a while, and when she returned he was asleep. But the sight of

[1] This version of a well-known incident is given by Mr. Paul Wittgenstein, who was present.

[2] Beethoven's last words were very similar. It is odd how the parallel insists on cropping up.

the ravaged face overcame her. She gave an audible sob, and Brahms awoke. He gazed at her sadly, tried vainly to raise himself and speak. A tear ran down his cheek, and he was dead. It was a little before nine o'clock on the morning of 3rd April 1897, a month and four days before his sixty-fourth birthday.

Of his funeral obsequies, of the honour paid him by Vienna and all the musical world when they laid him by Beethoven and Schubert, there is no need to speak. He cared nothing for pomp and circumstance—though he would have been glad to know that Alice Barbi was there and that Dvořák was among the torch-bearers. Nor would he have been much interested in the monuments to his memory that arose with the years in many German cities—though some of them might have made him smile. But he would have liked to be present at the unveiling of the Meiningen monument in 1899: not for the monument itself, nor even for the panegyric pronounced, though this was 'among the noblest tributes ever paid by one man to another.'[1] Not these but the orator would have touched his heart, and the sentiments that brought the orator to that place at that time. For it was Joseph Joachim who spoke, and it was thus that he claimed once more the lost friend of his youth.

[1] Fuller-Maitland's phrase.

# CHAPTER V

## THE MAN

BRAHMS was short, about the same height as Beethoven (five feet five inches). His hair was fair, and he had a pair of very bright blue eyes which he fixed on you when he spoke with an intentness that was sometimes disconcerting. In early youth he is said to have been slender, and people who met him in 1853 or the years immediately following commented on his high voice and the immaturity of his appearance—an impression that is confirmed by an early portrait. The high voice persisted, much to his distress, and his gruffness in later life was often due to his attempts to force it down. His features, however, soon set in a more definite mould, and his form filled out. In his early thirties he was not an ill-looking young man, thick-set, with a noble forehead and a firm chin, though his slightly protruding lower lip gave him rather a scornful expression. The beard that he grew in 1878 changed his appearance considerably, and towards the end of his life he became very fat. He aged early. Soon after fifty he was getting grey, and in his last years he seemed an old man, though (until his final illness) his health was always excellent.

A certain picturesque untidiness that grew on him with advancing years he achieved more by accident than design. There were indeed exceptional occasions in later life when he would take a childish pleasure in dressing up for an official function and wearing all his orders, though even then he habitually wore a made-up tie with his evening dress and was liable to make odd mistakes.[1] But, while his linen was always scrupulously clean,

[1] The Duke of Meiningen presented him with two orders at different times, one much more important than the other. When dining at the court Brahms invariably wore the inferior order, either because he thought it looked nicer or (more likely) from sheer thoughtlessness. The duke knew his man, and no comment was ever passed.

he had a hearty dislike for stiff collars and smart new clothes for ordinary wear. A certain brown overcoat of his came in time to be regarded as one of Vienna's ancient monuments, and a plaid that he sported at Thun in the 1880s is said to have looked even more remarkable. His soft hat was often fit only for a scarecrow, but as he always carried it in his hand what did that matter? His clothes were much patched, and he insisted on wearing his trousers unfashionably short. When his long-suffering tailor at last defied his instructions and lengthened the legs Brahms took it philosophically. It was so easy to get a pair of scissors and snip off an inch or two at the bottom.

He never forgot that he was a man of the people, and he took pains to see that others did not forget it. When his likeable, uncouth father visited him in Vienna he neither hid him nor apologized for him, but made a point of introducing him to all his grand friends. Quite genuinely he was proud of him. The composer himself was rather uncouth and he enjoyed emphasizing his uncouthness so as to make it plain that he was different from his companions. Strangers who met him in this mood thought him bad-mannered, and they were not wholly wrong. But they missed the point. Though the stories of his rudeness are legion, I cannot recall one instance of his being offensive to his social inferiors. On the contrary he had a passionate sympathy for the 'under dog' and the understanding that comes from fellow-feeling. His stepmother and her son, his landlady, Frau Truxa, the humble folk who looked after his wants on his holidays—these and many others loved him for his friendliness and true kindness of heart. All children adored him, for he adored them. In their company, and perhaps only in their company, the barrier of his reserve was altogether overthrown. He entered into their play without a trace of self-consciousness, and it was for himself even more than for the pocketful of sweets he always carried that they ran to greet him whenever the news came that 'the little round gentleman' was about.

He liked to lend others a friendly hand. Dvořák (another man of the people) owed almost everything to him; Grieg bore witness to his sympathy and encouragement. But the full story of his generosity was known only to Simrock, who managed his financial affairs and could measure the whole extent of his stealthy beneficence. When a person or a cause awakened his sympathy he grudged neither money, time nor trouble. The Vienna Tonkünstlerverein (Musicians' Society) was a sort of musical club where musicians could meet informally. As soon as its formation was proposed Brahms threw himself into the project heart and soul, and when they made him honorary president he took his responsibilities very seriously, seldom missing the Monday evening meetings unless he was absent from Vienna. On one occasion Adele Radnitzky-Mandlick, a pupil of Epstein's, arrived at the club, but seeing only men's coats in the hall, and being shy of intruding, was preparing to depart, when Brahms happened upon her and insisted on her coming in. 'You'll sit between Epstein and me,' he said, 'and be our guest the whole evening.' After the session they went to a small restaurant where Epstein was standing host. Brahms whispered in Miss Mandlick's ear: 'You order just what I tell you.' On his instructions therefore she asked for all sorts of expensive delicacies. Neither she nor Epstein was much disturbed, since such rare dishes would certainly not be available in the humble establishment of their choice, and the horror of both host and guest may be imagined when the order was accepted and the delicacies began to appear. In the end it turned out that Brahms had ordered the whole meal in advance from a neighbouring hotel—and paid for it. It is an odd story of genuine goodwill and clumsy tactlessness.[1] A man of the world would never have allowed his guests to suffer such anxiety and dismay. But then a man of the world might never have had the kindly impulse that gave rise to the whole thing.

Brahms never acquired polish. One is tempted to say that he

[1] Mr. Paul Wittgenstein, who tells the story, considers my judgment too harsh and assures me that Miss Mandlick never thought of the episode save as a harmless practical joke. The reader must decide.

disdained to acquire it. But he had a well-stocked mind and could be an agreeable and interesting companion. His humble origin, the shortness of his time at school, his ignorance of the French and English languages must not lead us into the error of imagining that he was ill-educated. From his earliest years he was an enthusiastic, intelligent and diverse reader. The few books he purchased as a boy out of his meagre savings grew into a library of which the elderly master was justly proud. Besides the extensive musical section that included a number of rare editions and such treasures as Mozart's autograph manuscript of the great G minor Symphony, it contained a big literary section, in which could be found a good collection of the best German authors in verse and prose and a representative selection of works on history, politics and philosophy. Among Brahms's friends were numbered such men as Hanslick, Spitta, Pohl, Billroth and Widmann, and he could meet them with a background of general knowledge comparable to their own. In the society of men of culture he was happy and he enjoyed the give-and-take of a lively discussion.

With strangers he often appeared to less advantage, for he was shy and *gauche* and he did not suffer fools gladly. Always he was on the alert for any insincerity, any attempt to lionize him, and quick to check it with a crushing retort. It was this kind of thing that won him the reputation outside his own circle of being (in Miss May's words) 'difficult, sarcastic and arrogant.' He was quite aware of what people thought, but it is not apparent that he made much effort to amend his ways.

If only this were all! But even his friends were not immune from unprovoked attacks. An outburst might occur at any time. The man had a devil in his tongue that he was often (and especially in his later years) unable to control. There was the celebrated occasion when, after horrifying a gathering of friends with a series of offensive remarks, he got up and left the room, only stopping at the door to say: 'If there is any one here whom I have not insulted, I beg his pardon.' Here is no question of mere tactlessness. He knew just what he had done, and there is nothing to be said except that he lost his temper. His admirers can only regret that the man who was at heart so generous, so kind, was also capable of rudeness, even downright cruelty, to people who had done nothing to deserve it, that he could make his friends suffer for no better reason than the satisfaction of a twisted sense of humour, and that he could, though more rarely, stoop to sheer spite and vindictiveness.[1] Darkest of all is the small group of stories of which his tirade against women (described earlier in this volume) is an example.[2] With such faults as these, combined with a reluctance to admit himself in the wrong and a genius for writing letters susceptible of fatal misconstruction, we cease to be surprised that he lost friend after friend and gained an unenviable name as an ill-natured bear.

In an interesting passage in her *Impressions that Remained* Dame Ethel Smyth discusses Brahms's attitude to women. He had, she thinks, little respect for them, regarding them as mere play-things and holding a poor opinion of their intellectual capacities. There is a good deal to be said for this judgment, provided we make the obvious exceptions (as Dame Ethel intended we should) and confine it to the generality of women, especially young women. His introduction to female humanity at the Hamburg *Lokale* was not auspicious, and the girls who plagued him for autographs or hunted him as a lion after he had achieved celebrity would not improve his opinion of the sex. In sheer self-defence he could not afford to take them seriously, and he is not much to be blamed if he was abrupt in dismissing them when they tried to waste his time. One can understand that an endless series of incidents of this kind might drive him in the end to those rather undignified adventures in paid love that were an element of his later life in Vienna. One begins to see, too, how it was that this man who

[1] See, for instance, his sorry behaviour with regard to the *Putzmacherin* letters described by Ernest Newman in an appendix to the third volume of his *Life of Richard Wagner*.

[2] See *supra*, pp. 6–7.

so often complained of loneliness, so often talked of his longing for a wife and a home, and who so adored children, remained nevertheless a bachelor.

His own explanation that at the time he thought of marriage he was too poor to afford it simply won't do. Even in the Göttingen days, when he was wooing Agathe von Siebold, his prospects were far better than ever his father's had been—and they soon got better still. It is much more likely that he feared the effect on his composition of family cares and responsibilities. Even more perhaps he shied away from the idea of giving hostages to a woman. As he once wrote to Widmann, he could not bear the idea of having in the house a woman who had a right to be kind to him, to comfort him when things went amiss. The mere suggestion of patronage from a member of what he regarded as the inferior sex was disgusting to him; nor does the idea of a wife who would be a true and worthy helpmate seem ever to have occurred to him. Perhaps it is as well he did not marry. He would have made an intolerable husband.

To feminine charm he was by no means impervious. His sensibilities were touched in turn by Agathe von Siebold, Luise Dustmann, Elisabeth von Herzogenberg, Hermine Spies and Alice Barbi—perhaps too by Julie Schumann, Clara's daughter. But the best of these, Julie and Elisabeth, were inaccessible. With the others he only philandered (dangerously in the case of Agathe). They were among the pleasures, not the essentials of life, and his sentimental relations with them are of little importance in an estimate of his character.[1] We must remember, however, that his dealings with women were not exclusively sentimental, and that a gifted woman could generally command the respect he withheld from her less talented sisters. No doubt he found Elisabeth von Herzogenberg attractive; but their friendship rested on the surer ground of his admiration for her remarkable musical gifts and critical insight. His sincere attachment to Amalie Joachim was

[1] Specht believes that he was in love with all the ladies I have mentioned. It depends on what one means by the words 'in love.'

entirely a matter of their common interest in Joachim and in music. He was at least as successful as most men in establishing satisfactory and quite unequivocal relations with the wives of his friends. Frau Faber, Frau Fellinger, Frau Engelmann and many others were all devoted to him and understood him well enough to overlook his occasional bad manners and unreliable temper.

We have not yet considered Clara Schumann. She was an altogether unique phenomenon in the life of Brahms, his inspiration and ideal, the shining antithesis to the girls of the *Lokale*. Despite his extreme youth his early love for her was deep and whole-hearted, the supreme experience of his life, compared to which his subsequent flirtations were mere shadows. After the understanding of 1856 no word of passion passed between them, but they remained loyal and devoted friends till her death. It was not always easy. Brahms's pen was clumsy. Clara, with her deficient sense of humour, was sometimes unreasonable. When that happened Johannes would swallow his pride, take the blame on himself and sue for forgiveness as he would never sue to any one else. On 19th March 1874, when she was in trouble, he wrote to her: 'Let this deep love of mine be a comfort to you; for I love you more than myself, more than anybody or anything on earth.' That remained true to the end.[1]

Nietzsche, discussing Brahms's music, coined a famous phrase about 'the melancholy of impotence.' This accords well with Wolf's 'Brahms cannot exult.' Both judgments are prejudiced, both are excessive; yet they contain an element of truth and they have a bearing that goes beyond the music. Brahms was certainly averse from undertaking more than he was sure he could perform. He disliked any enterprise that involved much risk. The first signs of what ultimately became a really singular caution appeared early. Most students of composition treasure their early efforts unless (or until) they forget them. To find a boy systematically burning his own music, as Johannes burnt the pieces he wrote for

[1] Those who are interested will find a fuller account of Brahms's relations with women in Schauffler's *The Unknown Brahms*.

Marxsen, is altogether unusual.[1] It is as though he feared that they might somehow be produced later in evidence against him. As yet, however, this was merely an isolated symptom, only significant in view of what followed. Joachim and Schumann found no lack of generous enthusiasm in the young Johannes, and there is any amount of ardour in the early piano sonatas. Perhaps it was at the Altenburg in 1853 that he first discovered how unrestrained candour might be dangerous. But it was his next experience that really shook him and began to modify his character. For two years he loved Clara Schumann, loved her heart and soul —and in the end it came to nothing. He staked his happiness and he lost. Every one noticed that between 1854 and 1856 he lost much of his boyish frankness, grew quieter, more reserved. Then, in 1858, came the unfortunate affair of Agathe von Siebold and, in 1860, the no less unfortunate business of the neo-German school and the manifesto. Like every one else, Johannes had to learn by his mistakes. But it is a pity that every lesson should have taught him that the world is not to be trusted and that it does not pay to take a chance. Alike in music and in life the adventurous impulse was sternly repressed and the cautious element already latent in his character strengthened and encouraged. The effect on his music will be noticed in the next chapter. But his whole life was influenced. He began to fortify himself behind barrier after barrier of reserve and precaution. He could not say, like Beethoven, 'No man has lifted my veil,' because he himself in his unwisdom (as it seemed to him) had already lifted it. But he did his best to ensure that it should not be lifted again. He became abrupt and rude. He developed a disastrous gift for sarcasm. The frank passion of his earliest letters to Clara Schumann gave place to the obscure, twisted utterances with which in

[1] The habit remained with him through life. He made a point of destroying his sketches and such finished works as did not satisfy his stern critical judgment. The result is that his published works represent only a fraction of what he wrote and that he left very little unpublished music behind him when he died.

his maturity he habitually expressed himself when any matter under discussion went close to his heart. Having weathered the storms of his youth he was resolved that neither his emotions nor his enthusiasms should involve him in further catastrophic disturbances. He would undertake no enterprise whose end he could not foresee, no course of action whose consequences he could not control. He succeeded tolerably well. His life in Vienna was as equable as most men's; he realized his ambitions within the limits he set himself. The price he paid was loneliness of soul and inner discord. For the warm-hearted young romantic was not dead, only closely prisoned. He appears again and again in the generous benefactor, the children's friend, and he permeates, though he never controls, the music. In his latest phase it sometimes seems as though Brahms were inclined to allow the prisoner a wider liberty, and it is interesting to speculate what he might have written had he lived ten years longer. But in the ordinary affairs of life little change is discernible. Caution, at first a policy, then a habit, grew at last into something like an obsession. The bars of the prison had rusted in and he *could* not enlarge the prisoner. Therein lies the 'impotence.' To that extent Nietzsche is justified. There were two elements in Brahms's nature, one struggling to be free, the other bent on restraining him. The result was psychological conflict revealing itself in impatience, shortness of temper, and combining with other factors to produce those occasional scenes wherein he was so lamentably untrue to himself.

His cautious attitude to life accorded very well with his philosophy. At an early age Brahms lost his belief in the Christian God, and he never recovered it. His unconcealed scepticism was a grief to many of his more orthodox friends and wrung from Dvořák the cry: 'Such a great man! Such a great soul! And he believes in nothing!'[1] But it must not be imagined that he was indifferent or flippant towards the most serious questions that confront mortals. The stoicism with which he armed himself to

[1] See Alec Robertson's *Dvořák*.

meet the vicissitudes of life was not the kind of philosophy in which a light-minded man finds a comfortable refuge for his superficiality, but a bleak system that demands much of its votaries and offers little in exchange, holding that virtue is its own reward and death the end of all things. Stoicism is the key to many things in Brahms. It is as a stoic that he faced the Leipzig failure of his D minor Concerto in 1859. But those were early days, before his spirit was completely disciplined. Later he achieved a fuller control. One is struck more than once by the apparent callousness with which the master accepted the failure of a first performance or the loss of a friend of whom death or his own clumsiness had robbed him. He was not really indifferent. But he had schooled himself to accept the inevitable, to endure what he could not prevent. Right up to the end, however, there were occasions when the philosophical armour proved inadequate. The death of his mother, the death of Clara Schumann, touched him too nearly for him to be able altogether to conceal his distress. For that we like him the better.

The truth may be that his stoicism was an attitude forced on him by circumstances and approved by his reason, but never really compatible with his temperament. He tried his best, but he could never make himself into a complete stoic. The complete stoic must achieve absolute mastery over himself. That tremendous victory won, he can banish fear and meet what fortune sends with an equal mind. Brahms with his bad temper and warm heart was not cast in this heroic mould. He never entirely mastered himself, and as a result he was always vulnerable and sometimes afraid. In particular he feared death. This fear may well have lain at the back of his peculiar aversion to sickness.[1] Two of his closest friends, Billroth and Herzogenberg, fell ill in 1887 and never completely recovered. It is remarkable that from that year Brahms's interest in them wanes. He was not so heartless as to drop them altogether, but he no longer sought them out.

[1] The point will not bear pressing. Healthy men often dislike sickness.

Death himself was not so easily avoided, and Brahms had too much honesty, too much courage, to shun that encounter. On the contrary, he seized every opportunity to look his enemy in the face. If we except *Rinaldo*, the *Triumphlied* and perhaps the Alto Rhapsody, every one of his major choral works, from the *Burial Hymn* of 1858 through the Requiem, the *Song of Destiny*, *Nänie*, to the *Song of the Fates* of 1883, is preoccupied with the mystery of death and the destiny of mankind, and he returns to it once more in the *Four Serious Songs* of 1896. Such steady confrontation contrasts oddly with his request to his doctor during his last illness to tell him 'nothing disagreeable.' But the contradiction is not beyond resolution. When the time came for him to go out into the darkness Brahms determined to go with dignity, without heroics, above all without fuss. To sustain the long ordeal with never-failing fortitude required an almost superhuman firmness that was beyond him, and who shall blame him if once and again his will seemed momentarily to falter? But it became a little easier if he could pretend that he was confident of recovery. That pretence he maintained, successfully on the whole, till within a few days of the end. The true stoic of course needs no pretence. But the true stoic is seldom a very sympathetic character, and we feel drawn to Brahms by his very weakness and imperfection. Behind his stoic mask he was such a very human person.

# PART II

## CHAPTER VI

### THE MUSICIAN

It was inevitable that they should compare him with Beethoven. The same lack of inches, the same habit of walking with head slightly forward and hands clasped behind the back, the same love of the countryside, the same inveterate bachelordom, the same bad temper! Even 'asses' were bound to notice these things. In the same way even 'asses' could not fail to recognize his musical affinities. Up to the time he was twenty he knew very little of the work of contemporary composers. From the first it was Beethoven, Mozart and Haydn who attracted him, and his talent developed in conformity with his tastes. Not only did he display a remarkable faculty for thinking along a straight line, for getting the most out of a theme, but he had an exceptional gift for organization, an ability to see the whole wood in spite of the trees and a capacity for self-discipline altogether remarkable for a boy. By a supremely lucky stroke of fortune he fell into the hands of Marxsen with his profound insight into the art of both Beethoven and Bach. From him he got exactly what he needed. There was hardly another man in Europe who could have given it to him. With his own endowments fostered by Marxsen's training he became the man we know, the composer of sonatas, symphonies and chamber music on classical lines, as well as much vocal music. No one since Beethoven had produced anything like so large or so impressive a collection of pieces of this kind.[1] With a single exception [2] all the major instrumental works have three or four

[1] There is Schubert, of course. But Schubert is Beethoven's junior contemporary, not his successor.

[2] The F minor piano Sonata, which has five movements.

movements, and every one has at least one movement in sonata form. Of course Brahms is the heir of Beethoven. The thing is obvious and is not affected by any judgment we may make regarding the relative greatness of the two composers, nor by any consideration of that large part of Brahms's output wherein the influence of Beethoven is less apparent.

His own attitude on the subject was never in the slightest doubt. In the very first bar of his first published work, the piano Sonata, Op. 1, he nails his colours to the mast with a reference to the greatest of Beethoven's sonatas that is obviously deliberate:

In case that is not enough he modulates in the sixth bar from C to G major and then in the ninth bar plunges on to the chord of B♭, a remarkable procedure that has precisely one conspicuous prece-dent, the 'Waldstein' Sonata. There is a rather attractive swagger about the gesture with which he proclaims: 'Let others do as they will: *my* master is Beethoven.' 'Master,' be it noted, never 'forerunner,' never 'brother.' Brahms's critical discernment, supported by his genuine modesty, saved him from that mistake. His admirers were not always so wise. They spoke of 'the tenth Symphony' (with reference to the C minor) and of 'the three B.s' (Bach, Beethoven, Brahms). This was the kind of thing that enraged him and made him talk about 'asses.' Beethoven's heir he might be, in a modest interpretation of the term. His peer he was not and never claimed to be, and his supporters by their rash assertions only put him in a false position. The harm they did remains to this day. No one thinks he is belittling Schumann or Strauss by an admission that Beethoven was greater than either of them. But a critic has only to make a comparison between Brahms and Beethoven to the detriment of Brahms and the ignorant will believe that Brahms has been successfully 'debunked.'

Perhaps it will be as well to notice this misunderstanding at the outset and get it out of the way. Brahms's inferiority to Beethoven is not a matter of technique. In his powers of organisation, his faculty for expanding an idea, he is at least comparable to his predecessor, and in the art of contrapuntal manipulation he is undoubtedly his superior. The problem is more subtle than that, and resolves itself ultimately into a question of temperament—perhaps I should say of character. Beethoven was one of the most positive people who ever walked this earth.[1] He was not an orthodox churchman, but most certainly he believed in God. Even more certainly he believed in himself and his art. His music is all assertion, very often dramatic assertion, and his energy is volcanic. He loves to wander among the grandest of rugged scenery. Neither the height nor the steepness of a peak dismays him. He will fight his way by sheer resolution up slopes where no other dare follow; he will take risks, leaping incredibly over yawning chasms. Occasionally he moves in defiance of ascertainable laws, working a miracle that makes us gasp (as in the famous entry of the horn at the end of the development in the 'Eroica'). His endurance knows no limits, he always has power in reserve; he can exist for long stretches at altitudes which the rarity of the atmosphere forbids to lesser mortals.

In sheer endurance Brahms is something like his equal. Few Beethoven movements exceed the first movement of Brahms's first Symphony or the last movement of his fourth as regards this quality. Yet he never reaches the highest summits of all because in the last resort he believes neither in God nor himself. Lacking

[1] I refer to his beliefs and his music. His vacillations in dealing with ordinary day-to-day affairs are irrelevant to my point.

faith, he lacks confidence. He is too cautious, he will never risk a leap and chance disaster. He can cross a chasm at need, and the performance may be thoroughly exciting. But examination generally shows that where Beethoven dares everything and accepts the risk, Brahms has taken every precaution and the danger is more apparent than real. At the end of the slow movement of his E♭ major Concerto Beethoven arrives on his tonic chord, B major. The piano fades into silence and nothing is left but two bassoons holding an octave B. They fall a semitone, the octave is taken over by the horns. Then, after a pause, the piano re-enters on that astonishing chord of E♭ major. There is no further preparation. E♭ is taken as established and we proceed without more ado to the finale. But what happened on that A♯? By what mysterious alchemy was it changed into B♭, the dominant of the new key? What is the link? The answer is that there is no link. Beethoven has leapt:

Superficially there is a similarity between this passage and those bars in the introduction to the finale of Brahms's first Symphony that lead to *più andante*. Having deliberately obscured his C minor tonality Brahms reaches a diminished seventh on A♮. At this point he silences his orchestra. Only a low-pitched C on violas and timpani is left above the bass during its descent through A♮ and A♭ to G. As it reaches G the horn enters on E♮, the first note of his solo in C major:

[1] I write the bassoon notes in the second bar as A♯ to make the point clearer. Beethoven has B♭.

Brahms gets his thrill; there is no question about the dramatic force of the passage. But there is no mystery. He has taken no chance, made no leap. The progression from a diminished seventh on A through an (implied) augmented sixth on A♭ to a second inversion on G is a student's commonplace.

More usually, however, Brahms avoids chasms altogether. His genius is naturally lyrical.[1] Beethoven will stop his music in full flood to reiterate a chord in a series of dramatic hammer-blows, using rhythm alone to make his point. After experimenting once (in the first movement of the D minor piano Concerto) with this manner of utterance Brahms discards it almost entirely in favour of the more equable flow of long streams of melody or polyphony. It is a less sensational method, better suited to his cautious instincts, his distrust of extremes.

Caution grew on him as he got older. One can watch the process at work even in his *tempo* directions. The romantic, exuberant early works are full of *presto, allegro, molto adagio*. In his maturer music, while he does not altogether forgo very fast and very slow speeds, he shows a characteristic tendency to qualify, writing such directions as *vivace ma non troppo presto* (G major Quintet), *agitato (allegretto non troppo)* (B♭ major Quartet). In the second Symphony *allegro non troppo* is followed by *adagio non troppo*. Even the *allegretto grazioso* of the third movement must be qualified with *quasi andantino* and it presently gives place to *presto ma non assai*. The fast movements tend to become slower, the slow

[1] The point I make here I borrow from Neville Cardus. See his essay on Brahms in *Ten Composers*.

ones faster. Applied to the scherzo this process brought about a genuine innovation. In his earliest works these movements are headlong affairs in three-four or six-eight time on the model of Beethoven and Schubert. But the G minor Quartet, Op. 25, has for its second movement an 'Intermezzo' (*allegro ma non troppo*) and for its third an *andante con moto*. Of the two the *allegro* is more like a slow movement than the *andante* (which reminds one of the Minuet). Neither carries the title 'Scherzo.' In the G major Sextet we get another *allegro non troppo*, but now with the title 'Scherzo' and in two-four time. The later works afford many examples of this slow, typically Brahmsian type of scherzo or quasi-scherzo, sometimes in three time (as in the second Symphony), but perhaps more often in square time (as in the clarinet Quintet, where the speed has dropped to *andantino*). We have also to note a much faster type in square time. In the fourth Symphony this makes a joyous, full-blooded affair, but the scherzos in the C minor Trio, Op. 101, and the D minor violin Sonata are whispered softly with a faint undercurrent of anxiety. Some of the slower scherzos are joined to trios (often two trios) in a quicker tempo. In these cases a thematic connection is generally to be found between the slow and fast sections (second Symphony, clarinet Quintet). Occasionally, too, slow movement and scherzo are united in one organic whole (string Quintet in F major, violin Sonata in A major). These several modifications constitute an important contribution to the evolution of the sonata type of composition and supply a pleasant element of variety to Brahms's works in this style.

To sustain interest through four big movements by lyrical means, with the minimum of dramatic gestures, is possible only if full advantage is taken of flexible rhythms and contrapuntal opportunities. Thanks to Marxsen's teaching Brahms's art was grounded on Bach as well as on Beethoven. Even the early piano pieces reveal a contrapuntal way of thinking and a facility rare in a youth of twenty. Such passages as this from the C major Sonata, if somewhat less smooth than Brahms could write in his maturity, are nevertheless remarkable. One does not expect canons in the middle of an impetuous movement by a mere boy.

Johannes, however, was not satisfied. He embarked on a further study of counterpoint and emerged after three or four years with such a mastery of the subject as no great composer had possessed since Bach. The passage in the third movement of the A minor Quartet between the two sections of *allegretto vivace* gives a taste of his quality. First violin and viola play a canon based on a rhythmic modification of the *allegretto* theme, while second violin and cello present simultaneously another canon on the theme of the minuet. But to appreciate the full measure of his powers one should go to the Fugue in A♭ minor for organ or to the unaccompanied Motets. Fugues by augmentation, fugues by inversion, canons by inversion, canons four in one or four in two—every conceivable combination is worked with an ingenuity that recalls the masters of the sixteenth century. Inevitably the results are sometimes rather arid, and some of these pieces are perhaps best regarded as exercises in a technique that is to be put to more artistic uses elsewhere. To the man who had written them the fugues and canons of the better-known works must have seemed, contrapuntally speaking, the merest bagatelles. The true test of a contrapuntist lies, however, not in his ability to solve abstruse puzzles, but in the ease and dexterity of his part-writing. Perhaps the most difficult thing of all to achieve is a satisfactory piece in two or three parts. The slightness of the resources available put the severest strain on the composer's invention and contrapuntal skill. If Brahms has left us no string trios it is not, we may be sure, because he could not write them, but because he had a natural partiality for richer effects. For this reason his string quintets and sextets are on the whole happier than his quartets. But however ample the resources his chamber music never lacks transparency. In the whole of the G major Sextet there are barely a score of bars of full six-part writing; yet it could not be other than a sextet. The first movement of the same Sextet admirably illustrates Brahms's superb workmanship with its subtle interplay of melody with melody and the unobtrusive skill shown in the handling of the undulating quaver figure. Everything fits so perfectly that one can hear the piece several times before becoming aware of such ingenuities as this:

Unquestionably Bach and Beethoven are by far the strongest influences to be found in Brahms's music. Sometimes indeed he looks farther into the past. His keen interest in Palestrina and other sixteenth-century masters is very unusual in a composer of his date, and its traces are often to be seen in his vocal writing. But in emphasizing his classical orientation we must not overlook his romantic qualities. The group of artists assembled at the Altenburg in 1853 thought that in the E♭ minor Scherzo they detected a resemblance to Chopin's Scherzo in B♭ minor. Examination shows this resemblance to be so trifling that we may dismiss it at once. But it is significant that such a criticism should have been made, for it shows the sort of comparison that sprang readily to men's minds in those early days. It is not often now that we hear Brahms and Chopin mentioned together. Yet there it is, that romantic warmth that suffuses so much of the instrumental music and even more of the songs. We need not insist on the Chopin parallel. Schubert is much more important. Brahms admired Schubert profoundly, and the expressive melodies, the miraculously poetic modulations of the earlier composer find many echoes in the later writer's music. Schumann's influence it is the fashion nowadays to minimize. On the formal side Brahms was no doubt wise to avoid the very personal manner of his early patron; but passages such as these suggest that he owed something to Schumann in the use of sliding chromatic harmony and counterpoint:

The difference is that whereas Schumann often produces the effect of improvisation (and therein lies his charm), Brahms always knows exactly what he is about and where he is going. What he got from Schumann was absorbed and transmuted into elements of his own style. Nowhere is Schumann's spirit so clearly invoked as in some of the late intermezzi, the very music in which Brahms is most completely himself.

Geiringer is obviously right in regarding German folksong as the parent of the typical Brahms melody. Brahms's love for his country's songs was lifelong; he gathered them carefully and in 1894 published a collection of forty-nine that he had himself arranged. Some of his own melodies might almost be taken for folksongs did we not know their origin. Here is an example from the third Symphony:

Other tunes, such as that of the 'Ständchen,' Op. 106 No. 1, though a little more sophisticated, are clearly referable to the same source. Sometimes the line of descent seems to run through Schubert. The rondo tune of the B♭ Sextet is obviously a near relation of its opposite number in Schubert's B♭ piano Trio; but folksong is still the ancestor of both. When he wanted a touch of the exotic Brahms would often go to the gypsies for his models. The Hungarian Dances he only claimed to have arranged, though one or two of the melodies may be his own.[1] But he certainly composed the melodies of the *Zigeunerlieder* himself and the gypsy tunes that occur in the instrumental works (notably in finales). For the second subjects of his first movements he occasionally derives inspiration from the waltz or *Ländler*. The second Symphony provides the most famous example. In some scherzos, too, the influence of the waltz may be felt.

The story has already been told of Joachim's youthful motto F.A.E. ('frei aber einsam') and of the Sonata composed on it by Schumann, Brahms and Dietrich in 1853. Brahms decided that he too must have a musical motto and chose F.A.F.—'frei aber froh' ('free but joyful'). Both mottoes (but especially F.A.F.) crop up again and again in his music, a pair of innocent crypto-grams. F.A.F., it will be seen, constitutes an arpeggio on the triad with one note missing and, whether by chance or other-wise, represents a type of theme to which the composer became very partial. Of course every one uses arpeggio themes on occasion. Beethoven has one for his 'Eroica' Symphony and another for his ninth. Though generally less expressive than melodies based on conjunct notes, they lend themselves very readily to contrapuntal treatment. Perhaps it was this that influenced Brahms. But whatever the reason, his friends must

[1] It has recently been pointed out that gypsy music is not at all the same thing as true Hungarian folk music, and that Brahms failed to distinguish between the two.

admit that he grew rather too fond of his arpeggios. Consider the following:

Not one of these is a mere casual piece of passage work; each is an important theme and treated as such. Moreover I have quoted a mere handful of such types out of a total that must be very large indeed. There are instances—No. 2 is one of them—where original harmonization supplies an individual quality not in‑ herent in the arpeggio itself. But this is not always the case. In the instrumental music and the songs there are plenty of fine tunes to prove that Brahms was not lacking in melodic invention. But he fell too easily into habits, and of these the arpeggio habit is the most noticeable and the most unfortunate since it tends to obscure the individuality of the different works in which it occurs. But it is not the only habit. A good many of his second subjects in sonata‑form movements have a family resemblance, as if when he reached this point in a composition he fell almost automatically into a certain type of utterance, lyrical, graceful, sometimes rather square‑cut and generally in the major mode. He had an in‑

exhaustible supply of these things, and they came to him rather too easily. It is strange that with his critical watchfulness he should have failed to notice his tendency to overwork this particular vein.

Perhaps this is the place to allude to the charge of plagiarism so often levelled against Brahms. So far as I know it is always of melodic plagiarism that he is accused. Now the diatonic scale has only seven notes on which to ring the changes. Even when we take into consideration the difference between major and minor and all the transformations that varied rhythms can produce, it is generally agreed that casual coincidences amounting to three or four notes are not worth attention—unless the offender be Brahms. All eight notes of Beethoven's 'Eroica' subject, complete with rhythm, are to be found in a youthful overture of Mozart's; Bach's depredations extend to complete movements, and Handel is worse than Bach. We note the facts, remark on the absence of a law of copyright in Handel's day or on Handel's skill in rearranging the material, and consider we have said all that is necessary. But woe betide Brahms if we catch him with three or four of someone else's crotchets in his pocket! His own answer is a good one: 'Any ass can see that'; but it does not explain why the asses should bother—and they do bother. Is it that Brahms is so saturated with the classical tradition and the classical idiom that the listener's ear is constantly haunted by the flavour of something familiar and alert for anything that will give definition to the impression? However that may be, I think we must admit that had he been a melodist of the very highest originality, had he been free of the bad habits to which I have already alluded, the necessity to defend him would not have arisen.

In his dealings with rhythm Brahms shows an easy mastery that is equal to every occasion. Phrases of different lengths, phrases that overlap, the combination of melodic lines moving at different speeds—these are the stock-in-trade of the contrapuntist. Not that he disdains the square rhythm of German folksong in its proper place. The popular *Wiegenlied* is an instance of the magic that he (like Schubert) can work with the squarest of square patterns, four phrases of four bars each. But he was just as happy with three-bar phrases (third movement of the A minor string Quartet) and had a particular fancy for five-bar phrases (Haydn Variations, piano Rhapsody in E♭, slow movement of the A major piano Quartet). Combinations of phrases of different lengths are so numerous that it is needless to cite particular instances. But there is one place where he experiments so happily with an unusual rhythm that I cannot pass it over without mention. The slow movement of the C minor Trio, Op. 101, has the time signature $\frac{3}{4}$ $\frac{2}{4}$. This is not very enlightening. Actually the metre is seven, each bar of three being followed by two bars of two, and the natural division coming after the first three beats. The phrases correspond with the full seven-beat cycle. In my quotation of the opening of the melody I amend Brahms's time signature and replace his first two bar-lines with dotted lines:

After several of these seven-beat phrases he reaches the point where his melody must culminate and close. Probably most musicians would feel that a certain broadening is desirable here. But which of them would have hit on Brahms's method of bringing it about? He doubles each of the two unequal parts of his cycle; the original 3, 2, 2 becomes 3, 3, 2, 2, 2, 2. Stated thus the device has all the dullness of an exercise in arithmetic. Translated into music as Brahms translates it, it is manifestly inspired. During the two bars of three the melody soars as it has never soared before; during the four bars of two it sinks to rest in a cadence that is final. One has the experience, so rare in art, of a thought expressed completely once and for all:

Cross-rhythms are one of Brahms's habits, and his handling of them is most dexterous. Bars containing six quavers or six crotchets offer a temptation he can seldom resist to scan them both ways. (♩ ♩ ♩ ♩ ♩ ♩ or ♩ ♩ ♩ ♩ ♩ ♩.) Sometimes the change affects the whole fabric and is presented in successive bars, as in the Romanze for piano, Op. 118 No. 5:

Sometimes only one or two strands of the texture are involved and the contrasted patterns appear simultaneously, as in the finale of the A minor string Quartet:

Elsewhere the rhythmic conflict is more elaborate. The first movement of the G major violin Sonata affords an interesting study of some of the endless possibilities, and here is a pretty solution of the three-against-four problem from the clarinet Sonata in F minor:

In marked contrast with the muddled effects produced by some other composers Brahms's cross-rhythms always 'sound.' Granted an adequate performance, the ear has not much difficulty in sorting out what is happening.

Concerning his harmony there is not much that need be said here. We may note a fondness for low-pitched passages, and if some of these sound muddy there are far more wherein he obtains a warm, luminous darkness of his own. We may draw attention to those solid, direct passages consisting mostly of common chords in root position which contrast so effectively with the more fluid, more chromatic style of most of his writing. The best known of these begins at the twenty-fourth bar of the second movement of the third Symphony, but there are other examples, the Romanze, Op. 118 No. 5, and the Ballade, Op. 10 No. 3. The last-mentioned is a very original piece of writing with the big distance between the hands, and I quote the beginning of it:

His principal function, however, in the evolution of harmony was not to innovate but to classify, to codify. He was the lawgiver. What Schubert and Schumann had discovered by intuition in the realms of modulation, chromatic harmony and chromatic counterpoint Brahms, with his superior logical faculty, was able to fit into the harmonic system of the classical masters, thereby enlarging the resources of that system and making the new procedures available to all and sundry. To write a satis-factory textbook based on the practice of Schubert and Schumann would be very difficult, but textbooks can be and have been written on the harmony of Brahms.

At a piano recital on 17th March 1867 Brahms astonished his audience by playing as an encore the finale of Beethoven's third Rasumovsky Quartet. It was a surprising feat in more ways than one, and I do not feel sure that it would have pleased Beethoven. In spite of his purism—and he was a stern purist—Brahms was fond in his youth of playing Bach's organ music in piano arrangements, and in later life he would introduce his own symphonies to his friends in two-piano versions. There were some odd hesitations, too, regarding his published compositions. The first movement of the D minor Concerto started life as a symphony; the F minor Quintet was a string quintet (with two

cellos) and then a two-piano sonata before it made up its mind to
be a piano quintet; the Haydn Variations were published by
their composer both as an orchestral work and as a piece for two
pianos; even the clarinet Sonatas appeared with alternative versions
for viola and violin. One cannot imagine Dvořák, Tchaikovsky
or Wagner displaying such uncertainty or indifference towards a
question of instrumental timbre, and I think we must admit that
Brahms was less sensitive in these things than most of his contemporaries. Form and colour are at the opposite poles of
music's world, and it is not given to many to excel, as Mozart
excelled, in both of them.

Brahms found himself both by temperament and force of circumstances the champion of form in a generation that was mostly
engaged in the pursuit of new possibilities of colour. He was
a conservative with his roots in the classics, living in a radical
world, and he distrusted innovation. He would not accept, for
instance, the new valve horns and valve trumpets whose exciting
potentialities were revolutionizing the art of scoring for brass, but
preferred the old natural instruments, accepting their limitations
for the sake of the more beautiful tone which he alleged (perhaps
truly) they possessed. Even the horn Trio is written for a natural
horn. With the trombones he is no less cautious. In eight of
the sixteen movements in his symphonies they do not appear at
all, and he never uses them in a concerto. Where they do appear
their function is mainly dramatic, and he is chary of introducing
them into a *tutti* merely for the sake of sonority. Similarly he
abjures for the most part Wagner's triple wood-wind and elaborate
string *divisi*. With the brilliant, rich, sometimes garish, effects that
Wagner employed habitually in the theatre and that Tchaikovsky
for one adopted for symphonic use, Brahms will have nothing to
do, regarding them as incompatible with his austerer style. It is
probably true that he could never have orchestrated like Wagner.
But since he never wanted to orchestrate like Wagner that is not
very relevant.

I must be careful not to give the impression that Brahms was altogether impervious to colour. That is not so. Such things as the long horn passage in the coda to the first movement of the second Symphony or the last dozen bars in the slow movement of the fourth show that within his self-imposed limits he was capable of imagining and realizing the most delicate colour-schemes when the occasion presented itself. This sensuous quality becomes much more apparent in his latest works and culminates in the sheer loveliness of sound that makes the clarinet Quintet unique among his chamber compositions, and in the mellow warmth of the writing in his last piano pieces.

One has only to compare these intermezzi with the early piano sonatas to measure the distance that Brahms travelled in a life-time. Here are all those piano idioms that belong to his mature style: the heavy, sometimes rough, but always sonorous, chord-sequences (Op. 119 No. 4), the widely spaced arpeggio figures with a note unexpectedly missing (Op. 118 No. 1),[1] those other more closely spaced arpeggios, mysterious, romantic (Op. 118 No. 6)[2]—and so on. But it is not such details as these that make these pieces the very quintessence of Brahms. It is not even the mastery of the material, the form, the counterpoint, though these miniatures are put together with all the skill and experience that went to the making of the symphonies and with no less loving a hand. Beyond all this we are aware of a change of attitude. Freed from the labour and responsibilities of large-scale composition, his life's work accomplished, he can afford to sit down and talk to us gently and wisely as the spirit moves him. He unbends, he becomes confidential, almost sentimental. The memories of his stormy youth have been softened by the years, and at last he lowers a little the impassable barrier of his reserve and reveals the kindly, warmhearted, romantic Brahms as he has

[1] Compare with these the F. A. F. themes quoted on p. 102.

[2] These very expressive and truly harp-like arpeggios were an early discovery of Brahms. See the slow movement of the piano Quartet in A major, Op. 26. They are not mere accompaniments, but special effects he reserves for the rare, appropriate moment.

never been revealed before—save in the songs only. It is noteworthy that in the intermezzi he is no longer haunted by the shadow of Beethoven as in his larger instrumental works. Beethoven wrote little instrumental music in the smaller forms; nor, since Schubert and Schumann, could any one take him as a model for song-writing. In his songs and smaller piano pieces therefore Brahms can let his style evolve naturally without reference to anything but its own inner needs. His instinct for shapeliness can be trusted to see that every detail finds its proper place.

The Brahms of the songs and intermezzi is thus a less formidable person than the Brahms of the big instrumental works. It is tempting to regard this as the true Brahms, Brahms in mufti as it were, in contrast to the uniformed soldier who operates under Beethoven's orders in the symphonies. This is a view that must be allowed its proper weight, but it is only a half-truth. A man is what his nature and circumstances make of him. Beethoven and caution were in Brahms's blood no less than Schumann and the lyric impulse, and it so happened that it was the classic, conservative element that events combined to encourage, though never to the exclusion of the lyric element which is plainly visible in works of the sonata type as well as in the smaller pieces and the songs. To speculate what he might have become had he never heard of Beethoven, had Wagner been his intimate friend, is futile. He was as he was and as experience made him. Schumann's phrase, 'New paths,' was, as it turned out, singularly unfortunate. It was Wagner and Liszt who were to explore the new paths. Happenings that Schumann could not foresee were to foster a side of his protégé's character of which he hardly caught a glimpse, and it was as the upholder of law and order, the champion of the grand classical tradition, that Brahms ultimately found his place. That he could hold that place without pedantry, sustain his individuality and his freshness of inspiration without breaking very much new ground, is a measure of his greatness. If he never rose to the very topmost heights, if he is not to be

FACSIMILE OF HANDWRITING

AUTOGRAPH OF A PAGE OF THE ALTO RHAPSODY

numbered among the supreme heroes of the musical art, at least his good sense and modesty saved him from a fruitless assault on Olympus. Moreover he could boast, as not all the great ones he so sincerely revered could boast, that no tawdry, no vulgar music had ever come from his pen. He was an apostle of the middle way. The part he played was not sensational. His music lacks glitter. But glitter is no guarantee of solid worth. Cut beneath the sober surface of Brahms and you find true metal all through.

# CHAPTER VII

## PIANO AND ORGAN MUSIC

In this and the following chapters I attempt no more than a very summary review of Brahms's output. Neither formal analysis nor full critical discussion is part of my purpose, and I have not hesitated to dismiss a composition with a mere mention when I have had nothing in particular to say about it. Broadly speaking my arrangement is chronological, but I have freely departed from this where it has suited me to discuss works in a group, since the reader will find a complete list with dates of composition (so far as these are ascertainable) in Appendix B.

## PIANO MUSIC

THE FIRST PIANO WORKS. It is generally agreed that the earliest of Brahms's compositions to be published under his own name is the Scherzo in E♭ minor, Op. 4, which most authorities assign to 1851. An extended scherzo with two trios, it makes an auspicious beginning for the lad of eighteen, well made, vigorous, fiery and less difficult to play than the sonatas that followed it. The first of these, Op. 2, is a four-movement work in F♯ minor, composed in 1852. On the whole it is less interesting than Op. 4. Its best movements are the *andante* (a set of variations) and the scherzo based on a rhythmic transformation of the same tune. The Sonata in C major, Op. 1, was finished in 1853 and is far superior. It is easy to understand how this must have pleased Liszt at the Altenburg meeting, with its brilliant, opulent treatment of the piano, its orchestral effects and the meta-morphosis (quite in Liszt's manner) that the theme of the first movement undergoes in the finale:

But with all this Brahms justifies in four well-knit movements his declaration of allegiance to Beethoven at the beginning. In the F minor Sonata, Op. 5, he does even better. He wrote most of this in 1853, and it is tempting to think that here, for the one and only time in his life, he was affected by the spell of Liszt. The grandiose, rather theatrical opening of the first movement, the moonlit magic of the second (prefixed by three lines of romantic poetry), the interpolation after the scherzo of an extra movement entitled 'Rückblick' (retrospect) in which the slow-movement tune reappears in B♭ minor to an accompaniment of muffled drums—these, together with several details in the luxuriant piano lay-out, smack strangely of the Klingsor of Weimar. Geiringer, however, is of opinion that the second and fourth movements were written before Brahms met Liszt in 1853. Anyhow the Sonata, for all its youthful flourishings, stands firmly on its feet and deserves more popularity than it has achieved.

VARIATIONS. Three out of Brahms's first four piano works are solo sonatas, the only solo sonatas he ever wrote. Having completed the F minor he turned resolutely in another direction, and of his next seven publications for piano six are sets of variations. The first of these, Op. 9, is upon the theme of the first of the 'Albumblätter' which form the second part of Schumann's Op. 99. Brahms wrote the work in 1854, at the time he was helping Clara to face the catastrophe of her husband's insanity. In this music he continues, as Specht puts it, 'to dream Schumann's dreams for him,' and it is full of affectionate references to themes by both Robert and Clara. Gone is the orchestral extravagance, the youthful exuberance. If the piece is still not easy to play, the difficulties now are mainly due to an increasing preoccupation with counterpoint. Three of the sixteen variations are in canon and several of the others contain contrapuntal interest. This interest is again apparent in the eleven *Variations on an Original Theme* in D major, Op. 21 No. 1, though less ostentatiously displayed. In spite, however, of the pensive charm of its eighteen-bar theme and its poetical coda, this music is not altogether convincing, and the same criticism applies to the *Variations on a Hungarian Song* in D minor, Op. 21 No. 2, which some authorities believe to be a legacy of Brahms's tour with Reményi in 1853.

The theme of the *Variations and Fugue on a Theme by Handel*, Op. 24, will be found in the second book of Handel's suites for harpsichord. But the few unenterprising variations that Handel added to it will not stand for a moment beside Brahms's master-piece. Here at last he produced a set of variations that is entirely satisfactory. He subjects himself to the most rigorous discipline, preserving Handel's eight-bar scheme throughout his twenty-five variations, in only four of which does he forsake B♭ major for the tonic minor or relative minor. Interest is sustained partly by the careful grouping of variations, by the placing of the three chromatic variations (Nos. 2, 9 and 20) just where they will tell most against the diatonic background, partly by an amazing resourcefulness in the treatment of the instrument, but chiefly by sheer fertility of invention. The final fugue comes near disproving Wolf's dictum, 'Brahms cannot exult.' It may not be the most lofty kind of exultation, but here at any rate is a thoroughly eupeptic giant rejoicing grandly in his strength.

In February 1854, just before he threw himself into the Rhine, Schumann was engaged in writing variations on a theme in E♭ major that he believed he had received from the spirits of Schubert and Mendelssohn. This is the theme that Brahms took in 1861 (after he had finished the Handel Variations) for his *Variations for Four Hands on a Theme by Robert Schumann* (Op. 23). There are many 'Schumannisms,' and the funeral march at the end makes the composer's purpose unmistakable. The music is not difficult to play, but less interesting than the Handel set.

Having solved his formal problem with the Handel Variations Brahms amuses himself in the *Variations on a Theme by Paganini*, Op. 35, in devising two sets wherein virtuosity is the first con-sideration. His theme is that of Paganini's twenty-fourth Caprice on which Liszt wrote a study. But here Brahms puts Liszt altogether in the shade. Clara Schumann called them 'witch-variations' and lamented that they were beyond a woman's strength—but she did not bargain for the physique of the modern lady pianist. The habit of playing both books together at the same recital is tiresome. They are separate works.

BALLADES, OP. 10. By grouping together the sets of variations I have been compelled to pass over the four *Ballades*, most romantic, most popular and least difficult of the early works. Brahms has given us nothing more Schumannesque than these pieces. Even their form is unusually loose, recalling the patchwork of independent ideas that goes to the making of, say, a 'Phantasiestück.' But Schumann could never have contrived the powerful, fierce climax of the first Ballade, a dramatic musical counterpart of the Scottish ballad, 'Edward.' No. 2 is less successful; its F.A.F. theme lacks rhythmic impulse. But No. 3, a picturesque elfin piece, is highly effective when played with sufficient lightness of touch. In No. 4 we are dreaming Schumann's dreams again, listening to those characteristic inner voices.

WALTZES FOR FOUR HANDS, OP. 39. In these pieces, so simple to play and delightful to hear, we have the popular Brahms, Brahms *pandemos* as opposed to the Brahms *ouranios* of the symphonies. They have little in common with Johann Strauss and still less with Chopin. Most of them belong to the *Ländler* type, and if they have a model it is Schubert. The last is unexpectedly written in double counterpoint — and none the worse for that.

SMALLER PIECES FOR PIANO. After the Paganini Variations of 1866 Brahms published no piano solo for thirteen years. As his style matured he found other means of expression for his larger ideas, but discovered a new use for the piano as the vehicle for short, whimsical fancies. Gradually, however, this whimsical element gives place to a deeper, more expressive and intimate type of utterance till we reach those last pieces wherein 'even one listener is too many.' Too much store should not be set on the varying titles of these pieces; the rhapsodies are not particularly rhapsodical, the capricci not particularly capricious. But we may observe that intermezzi are generally slow, capricci generally fast, rhapsodies on a somewhat larger scale than the rest.

The *Eight Piano Pieces*, Op. 76, were published in 1879. First stands a Capriccio in F♯ minor, full of canons and inversions, rather a bleak affair and difficult. Next comes the B minor Capriccio, in which the gypsies make their one and only appearance in the piano solos. It is odd how few pianists notice that it is marked *allegretto non troppo*. In the beautiful and picturesque Intermezzo in A♭ major (No. 3) is heard for the first time the rich lyrical note of the later intermezzi. The fourth piece, another Intermezzo, is reminiscent of Mendelssohn, though more resourceful than Mendelssohn in its harmony. No. 5 (Capriccio) is fiery, full of cross-rhythms and difficult. Once more there is an echo of Mendelssohn in the gentle, lyrical No. 6 (Intermezzo), and of Schumann in No. 7 (Intermezzo) with its romantic tunes and sectional treatment. No. 8 (Capriccio) is sparkling and brilliant, with a magical moment of *adagio* before the end.

The *Two Rhapsodies*, Op. 79, are impetuous pieces recalling (in the words of Billroth) 'the young heaven-storming Johannes,' though on the formal side they are admirably disciplined. In the B minor Rhapsody a melodious interlude in B major and a poetic coda contrast with the prevailing mood, but the G minor drives straight through from beginning to end. Those who regard Brahms as conventional may ponder the very enterprising modulations at its start and ask themselves how the composer contrives to establish his key so securely without sounding a G minor chord till the eleventh bar—just before he starts moving towards his second subject.

THE LAST PIECES. We have now reached those ripest products of Brahms's genius to which I have already several times referred. Why he should have called the Op. 116 pieces *Fantasias* is not clear, for they are all capricci or intermezzi. No. 1 is a vigorous Capriccio of the concert-study type, uncompromising, full of octaves and brusque chords. No. 2 (Intermezzo) is whimsical with a fantastic middle section. No. 3 (Capriccio) begins and ends passionately, with a majestic episode in between. In No. 4 (Intermezzo) Brahms adopts a favourite plan of his, developing a piece of fragrant enchantment out of two trifling scraps:

He thought of naming this number Nocturne. The intimate mood is preserved in No. 5 (Intermezzo), a wisp of a thing that looks easy to play and is not, and in No. 6, the simplest of all the intermezzi and one of the most deeply felt. To wind up comes a Capriccio, fast and restless, with characteristic cross-rhythms.

Over the first of the *Three Intermezzi*, Op. 117, Brahms inscribed a couple of lines from *Lady Anne Bothwell's Lament*. The piece is a lullaby, its melody effectively placed in a middle part. Between the two stanzas is set a graver, more thoughtful episode. Over No. 2 hangs an atmosphere of sweet seriousness. The piece is in sonata form with a second subject that is derived from the first subject. In No. 3 the colours are even darker, and there is an undercurrent of anxiety.

The *Six Piano Pieces*, Op. 118, open with a passionate Intermezzo that seems to start in F major and only at the end commits itself definitely to A minor. This is followed by a serene, lyrical Intermezzo, evolved with an effect of complete spontaneity out of its first three notes. Next comes a Ballade in G minor, vigorous and rhythmic, with a tripping melody in B major for contrast. No. 4 (Intermezzo) is rich in canons but somewhat dour. No. 5 (Romanze) carries its double counterpoint more graciously and includes some playful variations on a theme only four bars long. In No. 6 Brahms creates the most dramatic and tragical of his intermezzi out of a bleak little theme that uses only three notes.

There is a tradition that this material was originally intended for the slow movement of a fifth symphony.

'A grey pearl—veiled and very precious,' is Clara Schumann's description of the B minor Intermezzo that stands first among the *Four Piano Pieces*, Op. 119. It is a true *adagio* with drooping arpeggios and hesitating syncopations. The querulous theme of No. 2 (Intermezzo) transforms itself most unexpectedly into a graceful *Ländler* and then resumes its former shape:

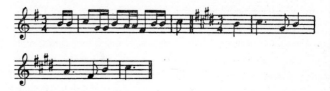

There is a gentle gaiety about the third piece (Intermezzo), and a fountain with graceful jets of spray. At the end of the set Brahms places a Rhapsody in E♭, as extensive and vigorous as those of Op. 79, but more episodical in style. It opens heroically in E♭ major, but works round to a passionate close in E♭ minor.

FUGITIVE PIECES AND PIANO ARRANGEMENTS. A full list of these will be found in Appendix B. Here I shall notice only the Hungarian Dances for four hands. Two books of these were issued in 1869, two more in 1880, and the composer subsequently made arrangements of some of them both for piano solo and for orchestra. In his letter to his publisher he expressly disclaims authorship of the melodies, which he describes as 'genuine gypsy children,' making apparently no distinction between 'Hungarian' and 'gypsy.' The well-known music itself requires no comment.

### ORGAN MUSIC

All Brahms's small output of organ music reflects the influence of Bach. The early pieces we may pass over except, perhaps, the dignified and highly ingenious Fugue in A♭ minor published in

BRAHMS AT THE PIANO
*A drawing by Willy von Beckerath*

1864. But the Eleven Chorale Preludes, which he completed at Ischl in 1896, and which were published posthumously, have the beauty and significance that belong to all his latest work. The shades of evening are falling, and though the rays of the setting sun break through in such numbers as the deliciously fresh 'Es ist ein Ros' entsprungen,' yet most of the music expresses a graver mood. Brahms is preoccupied even more than usual with thoughts of death, as is evident from the mere titles of most of the pieces. They breathe a sorrowful resignation well typified in the last (and perhaps the loveliest) of the set, 'O Welt, ich muss dich lassen,' with its beautiful double echo effect. Here is his final word to humanity, a touching and worthy farewell.

# CHAPTER VIII

## CHAMBER MUSIC

THERE is good reason to believe that the existing chamber music by Brahms represents a mere fraction of what he wrote. Still, the twenty-four works that he allowed to reach the publisher afford a more comprehensive view of his artistic development than can be obtained from either the orchestral or the piano music. All but four of the orchestral pieces belong to the single period of twelve years that stretches from the first Symphony to the double Concerto, and even in the piano works there is that gap from 1866 to 1879. Moreover, the later piano compositions are all on a small scale. But every one of the chamber music works is in sonata style with three or four movements, and they extend from the B major Trio of 1854 to the clarinet Sonatas of 1894. There are gaps, but no gap is greater than six years.

First on the list should stand a Sonata for violin and piano which Schumann approved and which Brahms intended for publication with the first batch of piano pieces. But the manuscript of this got lost, no one knows how. Next comes the composite 'F.A.E.' Sonata of 1853 for the same two instruments.[1] Joachim, to whom the Sonata belonged, suppressed three movements, but allowed the publication of Brahms's scherzo after its composer's death. The hastily written occasional piece now goes under the name of 'Sonatensatz' and we may dismiss it with William Murdoch's comment: 'Good fun—and harmless.'

PIANO TRIO IN B MAJOR, Op. 8. This, his first full-scale chamber work still extant, Brahms published in 1854. But some whim induced him to revise it in 1891, and it is the later, more concise and much improved version that is now generally played. All four movements retain the same tonic, a procedure for which there is abundant classical precedent; but it is somewhat unusual for a piece of this kind to start in the major and end in the minor.

[1] See p. 14.

We may notice the long melody that takes the place of a first subject in the opening movement, experiments in the *adagio* with the disposition of the instrumental forces and the graceful waltz that Brahms writes as a trio to his headlong scherzo.

STRING SEXTETS (OP. 18 IN B♭ MAJOR AND OP. 36 IN G MAJOR). The B♭ Sextet is a product of the Detmold-Hamburg period and was composed in 1859–60; the G major was written in 1864–5. But, as so often with Brahms, this only means that the bulk of the work was done in these years. He quotes the theme of the variations of the G major in a letter to Clara Schumann of 7th February 1855, and we know that this same G major was associated in his mind with the Agathe von Siebold episode of 1858–9. Up to a point, at any rate, the two Sextets seem to have progressed side by side. No special significance need be attached to the fact that there are several such pairs of works in Brahms's output. It was his custom to compose several works of a certain kind and publish the best of them, but it was mere chance that those which passed his scrutiny happened on several occasions to be two. More noteworthy is his choice of the sextet as the vehicle for his first published essays in writing for strings alone. The richness obtainable from six instruments suited his style. Not till later was he able to refine his thought to suit the more austere demands of the quartet. Besides, Beethoven had written no sextets; in adopting this form Brahms avoided the danger of a direct comparison. Apart from their firm construction the only obvious hint of Beethoven in these works is the tag:

which occupies the very same position in the scherzo of the B♭ Sextet as in the scherzo of Beethoven's fifth Symphony.

Of the two the B♭ is richer in effect. The easy geniality of its first movement is well indicated by the opening cello theme. There follows a set of variations in D minor, rather square in cut, and a headlong scherzo, very short. The final rondo recalls Schubert. Tovey calls the G major Sextet 'the most ethereal of all Brahms's larger works.' Perhaps the most attractive movements are a scherzo in two-four time that ambles along at a pace slow enough for us to savour the picturesque scoring in comfort and a set of variations on a very original type of theme in E minor. After groping for a while in the half-light of chromatic harmonies the music shakes itself free in a couple of vigorous variations and ends in a warm and serene E major. But it is invidious to select movements from a work that is consistent throughout.

PIANO QUARTETS (OP. 25 IN G MINOR AND OP. 26 IN A MAJOR). Both these Quartets were written in Germany and stand, in order of publication, between the two Sextets. The G minor is associated with Detmold, where a preliminary version of it was performed; the A major belongs to Hamburg. Both represent Brahms at his most expansive. Command of form is never in doubt, but there is a notable lack of the conciseness so conspicuous in his later works. This is most apparent in the first movement of the G minor, where the copious material and its extended treatment produce an exposition of gigantic size. Happily the composer's invention suffices to carry him from the bare, unharmonized opening through a lyrical second-subject group, a stormy development and a carefully varied recapitulation to a soft but unquiet close without loss of impetus. The contrast between the second movement (Intermezzo. *Allegro non troppo*) and the third (*andante con moto*) is of character rather than speed, the Intermezzo moving in a gentle twilight, the *andante* beginning somewhat in the manner of a minuet but subsequently developing an unexpected brilliance that is positively military. For his finale Brahms goes to the gypsies, writing a 'Rondo alla Zingarese,' electrifying in the rhythmic vigour of its three-bar phrases.

The A major Quartet is more orthodox, opening in a mood of classical restraint, though before the end of the first movement it develops a passion that is, as Tovey says, almost Wagnerian in its intensity. A mysterious passage with arpeggios for the piano leavens the long-drawn sweetness of the *poco adagio*. The scherzo is lively, its only blemish being the somewhat arid canon in the trio. But it is excelled in vigour by a finale wherein even the surprising breadth of the second subject hardly affects the over-riding impression of rhythmic urgency.

PIANO QUINTET IN F MINOR, OP. 34. This work had pre-natal experiences, first as a string quintet, then as a sonata for two pianos.[1] The first movement is powerful, majestic and intensely serious. But the second is tender, and its lulling rhythm carries a melody that recalls Schubert:

Brahms never wrote anything more exciting than the scherzo with its swift changes of mood and overwhelming climax. His finale opens with a dark introduction, but the clouds portend nothing more alarming than a sauntering cello tune, *allegro non troppo*. There is an odd, syncopated second subject and an enormous coda with a great passionate climax. I am told by a lady who heard Brahms play it that he took the *allegro non troppo* with extreme deliberation. Most modern combinations play it too fast.

SONATAS FOR CELLO AND PIANO (OP. 38 IN E MINOR AND OP. 99 IN F MAJOR). The E minor Sonata was published in 1866, but the F major is a much later production, belonging to 1887. Both give that impression of 'quality' that Brahms can always command, but they inspire respect rather than affection.

[1] Brahms not only performed the two-piano version (with Tausig), but published it as Op. 34A.

This is especially true of the bleak E minor, wherein the surly cello can seldom be coaxed up from the depths and every tune of all three movements is in the minor key. The F major (in four movements) is laid out with greater enterprise, and its first movement contains some bold experiments in tremolo for both instruments. But the most attractive movement is the slow one in the remote key of F♯ major. This is beautiful music in whose praise no qualification is needed.

TRIO IN E♭ FOR VIOLIN, HORN AND PIANO, OP. 40. Brahms's mother died early in 1865, the year of the composition of this Trio, and Specht may be right in regarding the *adagio mesto* as the composer's threnody for her—or he may be wrong. There can be no certainty in such a matter. But there is no doubt that the instrument for which Brahms wrote was the natural horn (*Waldhorn*), for he says so on the score. It is to humour this rigid instrument that he retains the same tonic for all four movements and forsakes in the first movement his customary sonata form for an episodical shape similar (as Schauffler has noticed) to that of the first movement of Beethoven's piano Sonata, Op. 54. Even so he sets the performer some problems. There is nothing that is impossible, but it is not often that the natural horn is asked to play in a key signature of four flats, as in the trio to the scherzo. There is a tradition that the original idea for the first movement came to Brahms in the woods at sunrise. True or not, it accords well with the romantic mood of the music. The scherzo is fast, the slow movement a dirge, and the finale clears the skies and provides the horn with plenty of opportunities to be its natural self.

STRING QUARTETS (OP. 51 No. 1 IN C MINOR AND No. 2 IN A MINOR; OP. 67 IN B♭ MAJOR). Brahms was in his forty-first year when he completed, in 1873, his first published string Quartet, the work in C minor. He declared, however, that he had composed a score of quartets before this and destroyed them. Furthermore, this very C minor appears to have lain on his desk a long time. Florence May is certain that it is the work he played to Clara Schumann in 1866 and Schauffler throws its inception back to 1859. I find it impossible not to associate this story of delay, patience and caution with Brahms's reluctance to face a direct comparison with Beethoven. The Quartet must be written, he knew, the comparison endured—but not before he was very sure that his work was as good as he could make it. That was characteristic of him. But no less characteristic was his refusal to evade the issue. In all his output it would be hard to find two movements more Beethovenian in their vehemence and concentration than the first and last of this Quartet. Intellectually his boldness is justified. Even Beethoven's music is not more remorselessly logical than this. But is there not a suspicion of self-conscious effort about the unrelenting tension, as though the composer found Elijah's mantle a trifle uncomfortable? The finest movement of the four is the *poco adagio*. Schauffler is probably right in finding in its middle section an echo from the Cavatina of Beethoven's Op. 130. But for all that the movement is pure Brahms, Brahms in his most romantic vein, scoring with an unwonted but happy picturesqueness. No less typical is the third movement with its uneasy, plaintive melody.

If Beethoven's shadow looms behind the C minor Quartet, the spirit of Bach seems to have taken a hand in the A minor, which is unusually rich in examples of contrapuntal ingenuity. In the first movement these are particularly associated with the first subject, whose 'F.A.E.' reference to Joachim becomes an 'F.A.F.' reference when it is inverted:

In the second movement a canon between first violin and cello with tremolo accompaniment produces a surprisingly dramatic effect, and in the third the melodies of the *quasi minuetto* and *allegretto vivace* are most dexterously combined in a canon four in two. The final rondo is a *locus classicus* for cross-rhythms.

Yet another influence is apparent in the B♭ major Quartet, composed two years later and published in 1876. Assuredly it was Haydn who hummed in Brahms's ear the opening strain of the first movement and suggested the fun that could be got by first contrasting and then combining rhythms of six-eight and two-four. There is not, it is true, anything particularly Haydn-esque about the song-like tune of the slow movement, but the influence is perceptible again in the third with its *Ländler* character and broadly obvious in the 'kittenish'[1] theme of the final set of variations. In the seventh and eighth variations figures derived from the first movement make their appearance and in the coda the main themes of both movements, one in two-four, the other in six-eight, establish complete mutual understanding and jog along contentedly side by side.

Having finally exorcised Beethoven's ghost with the B♭, Brahms wrote no more string quartets. To express itself comfortably his genius really demanded a richer texture than this form could conveniently afford, and his two remaining works for strings only are both quintets.

PIANO QUARTET IN C MINOR, OP. 60. This work was published in 1875, after the first two string Quartets, but before the B♭ major, and there is no doubt that it was during the years immediately preceding publication that Brahms completed it, for it is much more compact than the two earlier piano Quartets and bears other signs of maturity. For its origin, however, we have to go back to the dark, far-off time of Schumann's illness (1854–6),[2] and it is to this troubled period in Brahms's life that

---

[1] Tovey's word.

[2] See p. 21. As the Quartet now stands the first movement is in C minor, the slow movement in E major. But we know that the earliest drafts of the first movement were in C♯ minor. Did the sight of the first version on his desk give Brahms the idea of a key-scheme that

we must attribute its tragic mood. The sombre grandeur of the first movement is all the more impressive for the lyrical interlude provided by the second subject (which takes the unusual form of an eight-bar melody with variations). The scherzo, in C minor, is fast and passionate. In the E major *andante* the cello has the leading part, playing for the most part in its high register. Specht believes that in these fervent strains Johannes bids farewell to his love for Clara. The lightly scored finale is perhaps less interesting than the other movements.

SONATAS FOR VIOLIN AND PIANO (OP. 78 IN G MAJOR, OP. 100 IN A MAJOR, OP. 108 IN D MINOR). Brahms has written nothing more gracious than these three sonatas, in which he never seeks grandeur and woos rather than compels. The difficult problem of blending such disparate instruments as violin and piano has nowhere been solved more successfully than here, and the solution, as often as not, is the simplest possible, the violin singing the melody and the piano supplying the har-monies. Yet the pianist is never conscious of subordination, so varied and graceful are the figures of accompaniment, so dex-terous their manipulation, so resourceful the counterpoint. In the first movement of the G major (composed at Pörtschach during the summers of 1878-9) cross-rhythms are blended with an admirable lightness of touch. A deeper note is heard in the *adagio*, especially in the mysterious passage near the end. The three repeated notes with which the finale opens are an obvious reference to the first movement, but melody and accompaniment turn out to be those of the song *Regenlied* (Op. 59 No. 3). Later comes a reference to the tune of the *adagio*. At the end the major

---

might not otherwise have occurred to him, and are the remarkable allusions to the E tonality in the first movement afterthoughts to prepare the way after he had decided to transpose his first movement into C minor, but to retain the original E major for his slow movement? There is exactly the same sequence of keys (C minor to E major) in the first Symphony, but for many years the Symphony was growing side by side with the Quartet, and the one sequence may have suggested the other.

mode supplants the minor and the music melts away in a sky of cloudless blue.

Another song, *Wie Melodien* (Op. 105 No. 1), has lent its melody to the first movement of the A major Sonata, composed at Thun in the summer of 1886:

The reference occurs in the second subject and gives us all the clue we need for the mood of this most lyrical of movements, whose dreaming undercurrent comes to the surface in what Tovey calls 'the cloud-capped towers opening of the coda.' I find the second movement, a combination of *andante* and scherzo, somewhat less interesting, but the finale, with its very steady tempo and its predilection for the G string of the violin, is a worthy companion of the first movement.

There is a romantic melancholy about the *allegro* of the D minor Sonata (composed 1886–88). It starts with a great sigh and ends with an even greater one. In between there is considerable variety of mood, but the brooding element predominates, especially in the ruminating development (written on a dominant pedal throughout) and the coda (wherein a tonic pedal answers the dominant of the development). The *adagio* that follows is a simple, profoundly moving song giving us a glimpse such as is seldom vouchsafed into the warm, sad heart that beat beneath the composer's shaggy exterior. Hardly inferior is the scherzo-like third movement dancing on tiptoe through the twilight against a shadowy background. The finale is vigorous and full-blooded.

PIANO TRIO IN C MAJOR, OP. 87. This work was begun in 1880, finished in 1882 and published in 1883. Its first subject, though well contrived with a view to development, lacks (to my mind) aesthetic significance, and I cannot kindle much enthusiasm for the movement it introduces, in spite of an attractive second subject. The second movement, variations on a theme containing some characteristic syncopations, is more ingratiating, particularly the coda wherein the cello echoes the violin by inversion. In the scherzo, *presto* and mostly *pianissimo*, the mood anticipates the third movement of the violin Sonata in D minor. Tovey finds the concluding *allegro giocoso* 'full of humour and mystery.' Humour there is, of a typically German quality, in the odd galumphing theme, but too much of the music sounds manufactured.

STRING QUINTETS (OP. 88 IN F MAJOR AND OP. III IN G MAJOR). The F major was composed in 1882, the G major in 1890. They are the only string quintets that Brahms published, though we may remember that he *wrote* at least one other, the work that ultimately became the piano Quintet. At the beginning of the F major an easy-going melody, almost in folksong style, establishes a mood that carries us happily through the first move-ment without the need for any towering climax. The second movement, like that of the A major violin Sonata, is a combina-tion of slow movement and scherzo. But it is a far more significant example of the type. Its principal key is C♯ minor, yet it starts in C♯ major and ends, still more unconventionally, in A major with a very beautiful and most original cadence. Even Hugo Wolf, whose dislike of Brahms was notorious, acknowledged the power of this deeply felt, profoundly expressive utterance. For his finale Brahms writes a fugue that has some (but not all) of the *élan* of its prototype, the finale of Beethoven's third Rasumovsky Quartet.

He was fifty-seven when he finished the G major Quintet, but except in the assurance of the style there is nothing middle-aged in this music, which breathes the freshness of Vienna in spring-time. The opening theme starts low on the cello, and it is im-possible to make it come through effectively against the clamour of the upper strings. But Brahms was obstinate and refused to alter the direction *forte* for these accompanying instruments in spite of the pleading of Joachim and others. In performance some concession has to be made to human limitations. The composer seldom permits himself such violent contrasts as that between the carefree first movement of this Quintet and the tragic *adagio* with its extremely slow tempo, its bleak opening and passionate climax. Even in the waltz rhythm of the third movement we cannot altogether forget the catastrophe; there is a subdued, wistful quality in the melody. By the time he reaches his finale, however, Brahms has recovered his cheerfulness. Having solved the problem he has set himself by beginning in B minor a movement that is really in G major, he carries the work to a lighthearted conclusion.

PIANO TRIO IN C MINOR, OP. 101. Fanny Davies, writing in Cobbett's *Cyclopedic Survey*, gives an account of a private performance of this Trio at which she was present. 'A simple room, a small upright pianino, the three giants and Clara Schumann turning over the leaves. . . . I can see him now looking eagerly with those penetrating, clear, grey-blue eyes, at Joachim and Hausmann for the start, then lifting both of his energetic little arms high up and descending "plump" on to the first C minor chord . . . as much as to say: "I mean THAT."' So it is. Brahms knows exactly what he means and has learnt to say it with an incomparable succinctness. Such a stormy, romantic movement would have run to twice its present length had he attempted to get it on to paper in his earlier days. After this tumultuous exordium the second movement 'hurries by [as Tovey says] like a frightened child,' and again we find ourselves thinking of the third movement of the D minor violin Sonata. The *andante grazioso*, for all its formidable paraphernalia of seven-time and five-time, is one of the most serene movements Brahms ever wrote, a perfect lyric. With the finale, however, the storms of the opening are upon us again and work up to a furious last page that recalls the end of the F minor piano Quintet.

WORKS FOR CLARINET: TRIO FOR CLARINET, CELLO AND

PIANO, OP. 114 IN A MINOR; QUINTET FOR CLARINET AND
STRING QUARTET, OP. 115 IN B MINOR; SONATAS FOR
CLARINET AND PIANO, OP. 120 (NO. 1 IN F MINOR, NO. 2 IN
E♭ MAJOR). These four pieces were written at Ischl, the Trio and
Quintet in the summer of 1891, the two Sonatas in 1894. All
were inspired by the playing of Mühlfeld, the Meiningen clarinettist. The Trio is on a small scale and light in texture, the cello
spending much of its time in the tenor clef conversing with the
clarinet. In both the first and last movements the pair of them
introduce the second subject in canon by inversion. Contrapuntal virtuosity had become second nature to Brahms long
before 1891, and it interferes in no way with the flow of his invention. Yet it must be admitted that the Trio is not among the
most interesting of his compositions. Too many of its themes
are on the familiar arpeggio pattern; the signs of original genius
are fitful. But there is real beauty in the slow movement, and
the *andantino grazioso* disarms criticism with its innocent charm.

The Quintet is an altogether different matter. Many people
regard this as the loveliest of all Brahms's chamber works. If
we take the Handel Variations for piano as representing one side
of his genius, the master-craftsman rejoicing in his strength, the
austere classic for whom outlines must be hard and clear and who
has abjured the softer delights that art and life can offer, then the
clarinet Quintet is the obverse of the coin. Here all is warmth
and feeling. The music breathes a regret that is altogether
human for the passing of beauty, the mortality of happiness.
The kindliness, the love for his fellows that all too seldom succeeded in breaching the formidable barriers he had set up, find
utterance at last—and it is too late. He knows it, and his lament
is tempered with resignation. With all this there is a sensuous
element here that the earlier works lack, a sheer joy in the play of
colour that can be evoked from four stringed instruments and a
clarinet. This is nowhere more conspicuous than in the first
movement. The clarinet may soar over the strings, as at the
opening; it may contribute the dark, rich quality of its lowest

register, as at the beginning of the development; most characteristic of all, it may wander in the middle of the harmony, hardly discernible as an individual voice yet tinting the whole texture. But whatever it does it is always a live clarinet, never an abstraction.

During the first part of the *adagio* the music floats in an unearthly, moonlit loveliness. But then comes a wild rhapsody for the clarinet with tremolo accompaniment, a fantasy of almost oriental exuberance, quite unlike anything else in Brahms. This is the music Joachim had in mind when he wrote to Stanford: 'There is so much of the gypsy style in it.'[1] The passionate outburst subsides, serenity returns. But in the coda Brahms waves farewell —with infinite tenderness—to his friends the gypsies. The third movement opens quietly, and the atmosphere of restraint persists even when the pace quickens to a delicate scherzo rhythm. After such an *adagio* that is necessary. In the final set of variations one is struck once more by the sensuous beauty of the scoring, notably in the fourth variation. Ultimately the theme of the variations is blended (but not contrapuntally) with that of the first movement to bring the work to a tragic, yet quiet conclusion.

Though they are not to be compared in significance with the Quintet or even with the violin sonatas the two clarinet Sonatas make attractive music. The F minor (in four movements) starts somewhat gloomily but achieves a cheerful conclusion. The E♭ major (in three movements) begins gently, has an impetuous, scherzo-like movement in the middle and concludes with some simple variations. Neither Sonata is quite as innocent as appears at first sight. There are cross-rhythms, and canons lurk in unexpected places.[2]

---

[1] Letter of 16th December 1891.

[2] Brahms made two other arrangements of these Sonatas, one for viola and piano, one for violin and piano. The viola version is the more satisfactory of the two. In the arrangement for violin the composer's modifications extend to the piano part, and would-be performers must be careful to see that they have the appropriate copy of *both* parts.

# CHAPTER IX

## ORCHESTRAL MUSIC

'If he will touch with his magic wand,' wrote Schumann, 'those massed forces of chorus and orchestra and compel them to lend him their powers, we may expect still more wondrous glimpses of the spirit-world.' Johannes took the hint and wrote a symphony. It was never published, but its first movement became the first movement of the D minor piano Concerto, Op. 15, the whole of which (in the opinion of those best qualified to know) was completed before the Serenade in D major. Its unfavourable reception at Leipzig in 1859 we have already noticed.[1] The trouble is not difficult to diagnose. It was rash of Brahms to introduce himself as an orchestral composer with a work that plays for forty-seven minutes,[2] nor had he yet the experience to 'bring off' that immense first movement, bleak, tragic and full of dramatic gestures. Many signs of the novice hand are visible in the instrumentation. Strings are insufficient for so bold an opening; it needs horns at least. The scoring is often thick, the piano part lacks brilliance by the standards of 1859. Not yet were the Leipzigers prepared to accept the solo instrument as no more (in places) than an element in the orchestral texture. They were puzzled. Even a modern listener may take several hearings to get his bearings in this grand, dark movement, though he would probably be quicker than the Leipzigers to feel the charm of the second-subject group and the romantic horn solo. It is a pity, too, that Brahms retained both his tonic and his time signature for the slow movement. In itself it is a lovely *adagio*, but the first movement has surfeited us with those long six-four bars. The final rondo offers the variety we have been looking for. But Leipzig propriety was shocked to hear the unseemly strains of the gypsy band in the sacred precinct of the concerto. They had still to learn from Brahms what virtue was in the gypsies.

[1] See p. 25.          [2] Julius Harrison's timing.

The two orchestral Serenades (Op. 11 in D major and Op. 16 in A major) are called by Specht the 'Detmold Serenades.' Both were published in 1860. But the work in D existed as an octet for solo instruments in 1858, and Clara Schumann's letter of 20th December 1858 shows that she had already seen a version of the A major by that date. A revised edition of the A major appeared in 1875. Both Serenades are decorous, old-fashioned, not very characteristic. They know nothing of the storms of the D minor Concerto. The D major pays respectful homage to Haydn and early Beethoven. The A major is darker in colour, since it contains no parts for violins. One recalls the sixth Brandenburg Concerto and the first movement of Brahms's Requiem, wherein again violins are omitted, and wonders whether Dvořák had this Serenade in mind when he banished the brighter instruments from his own D minor Serenade in 1878. Isolated movements from both of Brahms's works are heard nowadays from time to time. But they are long, and conductors are seldom inclined to perform them in their entirety.

Brahms's next experience in orchestration was gained in writing the accompaniments to the Requiem and the choral works that followed it. He learnt a lot in the process, and it was with a much surer hand that he presently set to work on the *Variations on a Theme by Haydn*, which he finished at Tutzing in 1873. Full mastery is apparent here, and not only in the orchestration: the double counterpoint at the twelfth in the fourth variation, the imitations by inversion in the eighth, flow from his pen as naturally and easily as the purely lyrical writing of the graceful seventh variation, and the building of the finale on its ground-bass shows a fine combination of resource and imagination. Only at the very end does the bald restatement of the theme against a back-ground of diatonic scales strike the listener as rather a tame finish.[1]

[1] Later on Brahms used to make two-piano arrangements of his symphonies and play them to a select company before the works reached orchestral performance. We might guess that the publication of the Variations in a two-piano version was the result of his doing the same

BRAHMS AND SOME FRIENDS

Those present are (from left to right): *Standing*: Epstein, Mandyczewski, Hausmann,
Henrietta Hemala, Dr. Passini, Kruse, Wirth
*Sitting*: Fraulein von Miller-Aicholz, Hanslick, Brahms, Frau Passini, Joachim
This photograph was taken a few weeks before Brahms's death and

## The First Symphony

Although the C minor Symphony, Op. 68, was already well advanced when the Haydn Variations were composed, Brahms did not complete it till the autumn of 1876 (at Lichtenthal). This year marks the beginning of what might be called his orchestral period. Between 1876 and 1887 there appeared all the orchestral works we have not already noticed, the four symphonies, two overtures and three concertos.

In its intense concentration on a single mood of tragic striving the first movement of the C minor Symphony shows us Brahms at his most Beethovenian. Its inception, we must remember, goes back to the years of the D minor Concerto and his boyish passion for Clara Schumann. It is the feelings of those days that he is expressing, though the manner of their expression reveals his maturity. The music is almost all evolved out of a single theme, a strange theme, consisting of two simultaneous strands, one straining semitonically upwards, the other falling, also by step. Beethoven, we know, laboured long at his themes, but when they reach their final form they produce the effect of spontaneous invention. There is nothing spontaneous about Brahms's theme. Quite obviously it has been made—and how telling it is, just for that reason! For a parallel we must look not to Beethoven but to Wagner, whose themes give the same impression of being the final crystallization of a process of intense thought:

Brahms, 'C minor Symphony'

thing in this case and finding that the music went well in the arrangement. Unfortunately for this pretty theory modern research indicates that the two-piano version came first.

Brahms begins his movement ponderously, *un poco sostenuto*, above a steady drum-beat. When we reach the *allegro* the storm bursts and the conflicting scales strive furiously in a vast contest that even at the end remains undecided. The writing sounds thick at times, but now it is the thickness not of inexperience but of hard, solid thinking.

After such a mighty upheaval the short *andante sostenuto* in E major comes as a welcome relief. Towards the end its orchestration grows unusually picturesque for Brahms, who indulges in the rare luxury of a solo violin. For a scherzo he characteristically substitutes a two-four movement in A♭ major, *un poco allegretto e grazioso*, fanciful and graceful. But with the C minor introduction to the finale we resume the tragic mood.[1] These are extraordinary pages of an extravagant picturesqueness that (for the one and only time in Brahms's career) recalls Berlioz. Well might Elisabeth von Herzogenberg exclaim at 'the fabulous, roaring-lion basses after the *stringendo*.' The music is full of such portents. Most dramatic of all is the entry of the C major horn melody that disperses the shadows once for all.[2] The trombones enter at this point for the first time in the Symphony and presently announce a solemn strain that is to reappear once only, but with overwhelming effect, in the coda. Here it prepares the way for the broad melody that sends the *allegro* on its way rejoicing:

[1] That both the first and last movements of this Symphony have introductions is noteworthy. There are no introductions in the other symphonies, nor any in the chamber music, except for the finale of the piano Quintet.

[2] This passage has been discussed and quoted on pp. 94-5.

In the seventh bar the third bar of my quotation is repeated with the second D altered to an F. Brahms had a rude name for the wiseacres who drew unjustifiable conclusions from the chance resemblance of this passage to a similar bar in the famous tune from the finale of Beethoven's ninth Symphony. No one knew better than he the difference between Beethoven's tremendous affirmation and the pawky tune that presides over the altogether earthly joys of his own finale. But he gave us a fine movement, and his coda is as exhilarating as one could wish.

Most of the second Symphony was composed at Pörtschach in the summer of the following year, 1877. It is the largest of the four, and in three out of its four movements Brahms allows himself the luxury of trombones and tuba. But for all that it is the most serene and genial of symphonies. 'Brahms's Pastoral' it has been called. From the announcement by the horns of the gracious first subject (see example on p. 138) through the mysterious entry of the trombones to the frankly waltz-like second subject, the vast first movement unfolds itself with gentle ease. Even the intrusion into the development of a section in quadruple fugue causes scarcely a flicker in the barometer, and a dreaming horn enriches the coda with the sort of undulating melody that only Brahms could write. The slow movement presents us at the outset with two themes simultaneously and passes on to an unexpected fugato. Complexity is indeed a feature of the whole thing which, though finely wrought, moves one less than most of Brahms's slow movements. On the other hand no one will fail to respond to the appeal of the innocent oboe melody, the Schubertian changes from major to minor and back again in the *allegretto grazioso* that follows, nor to appreciate the delicate charm of the two *presto* sections even though he may not notice at first that they are both derived from the melody of the *allegretto*. The final *allegro con spirito* is the most closely reasoned movement of the four, full of inversions, augmentations, diminutions and the like. But these do not impair the robust vigour of a movement, whose parent, as the invaluable Tovey has shown, is the finale of Haydn's last Salomon Symphony, the D major.

Pörtschach continued to exercise a benign influence on Brahms, and it was there, in 1878, that the violin Concerto grew up with its smaller sister, the G major violin Sonata. The key of the Concerto is the same as that of the second Symphony, and there is an affinity between the first subjects of each work:

After a spacious *tutti* the soloist enters with a grand, theatrical gesture that recalls Beethoven's violin Concerto, and then settles down to open the exposition with superb dignity. Though difficult, the music is so free from the element of display that in early days it was called a 'concerto *against* the violin.' For this reason Sarasate would have none of it. But Brahms was writing for Joachim, to whom the work is dedicated. He often consulted his friend about his compositions, and such was his respect for Joachim's judgment that he would accept his advice on a point of form or style where he would brook no interference from any one else. On the other hand he would often, with his usual pig-headedness, reject suggestions regarding the lay-out of a passage for the violin, a matter wherein the violinist's opinion was most likely to be of value. Nevertheless there is little doubt that Joachim had a hand in the solo part of the Concerto, and Brahms repaid him by trusting him with the cadenza. Elsewhere in his works cadenzas are written out in full. Here only he is content with the old-fashioned pause and the direction 'Cadenz.' Joachim's cadenza is still the one most usually played. I have yet to hear another that will stand comparison with it.

At one stage the work appears to have had four movements. Specht quotes a letter in which the composer writes: 'The middle movements have gone and of course they were the best. But I have written a feeble *adagio* for it.' Few people will agree that 'feeble' is the proper adjective for this movement with its pure white light and celestial oboe tune. For his splendidly vital finale Brahms dons once more the gypsy's coat, a costume in which he seldom fails to appear at his best.

There is little display of academic learning in the *Academic Festival Overture* that he wrote for Breslau in 1880. But it is admirably suited to an academic festival with its large orchestra (the biggest for which he ever wrote), its tearing good spirits, student songs, vigorous rhythms and straightforward harmonies— to say nothing of that time-honoured joke with the bassoon. Lofty inspiration is not required here; only sound workmanship, and that is forthcoming. As a companion to this piece Brahms composed the *Tragic Overture* out of some material he had had by him for some time. I confess to a lack of enthusiasm for this work. There are one or two impressive moments, but much of the music is conventional in cut and fails to generate much heat.

Far more significant than either of the overtures, even if it does not quite achieve the Olympian heights of the violin Concerto, is the vast piano Concerto in B♭ major, Op. 83, which was finished in 1881 and published in 1882 with a dedication to 'his dear friend and teacher, Eduard Marxsen.' The work is neither so stormy as the D minor Concerto nor so serene as the violin Concerto. Its first movement starts majestically and ends triumphantly; in between the weather varies. We may perhaps notice the three long chains of trills for the soloist, a distant echo from the D minor Concerto, but in how different a context! The second movement is a novelty, an *allegro appassionato* in D minor, after the manner of a scherzo. Having made this excursion into a contrasted tonality the composer can return to B♭ for his *andante*. Here again the six-four time signature, the slow descending scale in a middle part at the opening and the shape of the piano figures in the twenty-fifth and following bars remind one of the D minor Concerto:

This is not to imply, however, that the movement lacks individuality. We must not forget the lovely and wholly original episode in F♯ major with great leaps in the melody and a far-flung accompaniment, nor the equally lovely duet for piano and solo cello at the end. In the final *allegretto grazioso* trumpets and drums are banished altogether [1] and the gayest of melodies goes dancing over a prattling semiquaver accompaniment. For the sustained lightness and brilliance of this music there is only one model—Mozart.

After a year or two during which he was mainly concerned with his last big choral works Brahms returned to the orchestra, completing the third Symphony in 1883 and the fourth in 1885. In the third Symphony he again uses trombones for three move-ments, but a double bassoon takes the place of the tuba. The bold version of the F.A.F. motive with which the work begins is a sort of motto for the whole symphony rather than the first subject, though it fits as a bass against the first subject as the composer immediately shows:

The reader must decide for himself whether this descending arpeggio theme is quite strong enough to carry the weight of a big movement and whether the second subject (which appears in A major and nine-eight time) is not rather short-breathed for a symphony. At any rate there is no doubt that Brahms built a

[1] The reader should perhaps be reminded that trombones and tuba are nowhere used by Brahms in a concerto.

fine solid structure on the foundations he chose. The present writer, however, gets more satisfaction out of the quiet *andante*, whose folk-like theme (quoted on p. 100) proves quite equal to the strains put upon it. Its second subject too has unexpected possibilities, the most remarkable of which are heard only when it reappears mysteriously, heralded by trombones, early in the finale. Instead of a scherzo we get the lightest of all Brahms's symphonic movements, a wistful little *poco allegretto*, economically but resourcefully scored. It is, however, in the passionate finale beginning in F minor that the greatest music of the Symphony is to be found. I recommend to every reader Tovey's analysis of this movement, which is far from simple. Here, for instance, are some (but by no means all) of the rhythmic changes undergone by the first subject:

At the end the *allegro* broadens characteristically into *un poco sostenuto*. The major mode is recovered. Above shimmering strings a horn dreams of the F.A.F. motto and the Symphony drops gently to rest on the sleepy wings of its first subject (p. 141).

Few movements in sonata form are so closely organized as the first *allegro* of the fourth Symphony (in E minor, Op. 98). The ordering of the diverse elements so that each fulfils its appointed function in the grand and intricate design is done with such unerring skill that the piece becomes a veritable *tour de force* of formal construction. From beginning to end the logic is in-exorable, and the amazing knot of imitations, canons and inversions in the development (before letter H) is only the supreme example of an intellectual pressure that never relaxes. That such concentration should not have stifled imaginative creation is a measure of what Brahms's musical faculty in its plenitude could achieve; for the colours, though never brilliant, are always changing, and the interest never flags. This fruitful alliance of heart and head is no less evident in the *andante moderato*. The C major opening of a movement that is really in E major, the anticipation (by diminution) of the second subject in the triplet semiquavers that precede it—these things reveal the hand of the master-technician. Yet this is as romantic, as richly coloured a movement as any in the symphonies, and its ending is as astonishing in its originality as it is convincing in its emotional sincerity.

The scherzo rejoices with a merriment that is almost Gargantuan, culminating in an exciting dominant pedal. When it is over the mood changes once more. In the theme of the finale, announced by the wind (reinforced for the first time in the Sym-phony by trombones), there is neither merriment nor charm, only power. Specht tells us that some years earlier Brahms and Bülow had been discussing the ciacona in Bach's Cantata No. 150. 'What would you say,' asked Brahms, 'to a symphonic movement built on this theme one day? But it would have to be chromatically altered in some way.' I quote Bach's theme and Brahms's modification of it:

On this basis he writes a colossal passacaglia, containing no less than thirty variations. To praise the beauty of some of these is tempting but unnecessary, since every hearer has ears. The truly impressive thing is the steady growth of the movement from climax to climax. Before the end we have risen altogether out of sight of the shady valleys of the *andante*, the cheerful merriment of the scherzo, and the wind roars unmercifully over the stony slabs of the vast mountain-side. It is an awful, heart-searching experience, a mighty assertion of the spirit of man.

Last of all the orchestral works comes the double Concerto for violin and cello in A minor, Op. 102, composed at Thun in the summer of 1887. It has a personal interest apart from its musical contents. 'This Concerto,' wrote Clara Schumann in her diary on 21st September, 'is in a way a work of reconciliation—Joachim and Brahms have spoken to one another again after years of silence.' In itself it is something of an experiment; no one, so far as I know, had previously composed a concerto for these two instruments. Brahms does not fail to make good use of the wide gamut they provide and there are effective passages of chord-playing for the pair of them together. Yet the piece has never achieved the popularity of the other concertos. The first movement that takes shape after a rhetorical introduction never quite catches fire in spite of its lyrical (though short-breathed) second subject. But the brief slow movement with its dewy freshness and cool melody cannot fail to charm. A merry, carefree finale with some exciting passages for the soloists completes the scheme. We know that Brahms had some difficulty in securing the required brilliance, and Geiringer produces a facsimile of one of the last pages of the score with Joachim's pencilled emendations of the violin part. It is amusing to find on turning to the printed edition that the obstinate composer once more disregarded the advice and stuck to his original version.

# CHAPTER X

## SONGS [1]

### §1. SOLO SONGS

SONG depends inevitably upon verse. Extensive cultivation of the German *Lied* only became possible when the romantic revival had unfrozen the springs of German lyric poetry. With all respect to Mozart and Beethoven the epoch of the *Lied* begins with Schubert's first really great song, *Gretchen am Spinnrade*, in 1814.[2] After Schubert come Schumann, Brahms and Wolf, and round these, 'the big four' of song as they have been called, are grouped a host of other writers of varying merit. Richard Strauss has endeavoured to carry the tradition into the twentieth century, but a romantic attitude has become more and more difficult to maintain in face of a changing world, and his has been a losing battle. The genuinely royal line ends with Brahms's *Vier ernste Gesänge* of 1896 and Wolf's *Michelangelo Lieder* of the following year. A single century includes it all quite comfortably.

Negligible exceptions apart, the big four set only German verse. Even the poetically sensitive Hugo Wolf writes his foreign songs to German translations. Similarly, on the musical side, they accepted the German tradition as a matter of course. Brahms's well-known 'Zigeuner' style is no more than a becoming fancy dress. No doubt this close concentration on a single line of development had something to do with the high quality of the work produced. But it was also responsible for a certain narrowness. Inevitably the same poets, the same poems were set again

[1] Brahms wrote about two hundred solo songs, not to mention the duets, quartets and folksong arrangements. Since it is obviously impossible in a small volume to examine each of these individually I have substituted the general essay that follows.

[2] This assertion was first made, I think, by Richard Capell.

and again; inevitably the same musical formulae kept recurring.
Mozart closes the vocal part of 'Porgi amor' (in *Figaro*) with:

O mi la . scia al - men ıno - rir.

The same cadence crops up again in Schubert's *An die Musik*:

Du hol - de Kunst,____ ich dan - ke dir.

When Brahms gets hold of it in *Wie bist du, meine Königin* (Op. 32
No. 9) he modifies it to accommodate the chord of the dominant
ninth:

Won - ne, won - ne - voll!

and in this form it appears once more at the end of the last of the
*Vier ernste Gesänge* (Four Serious Songs, Op. 121). By such
unconscious signs he shows how firmly rooted his art was in
tradition.

Richard Capell has remarked that the *Lied* was born of the
union of German lyric poetry with the keyboard style evolved by
Mozart and Beethoven. It is a pity that the biological metaphor
does not permit us to add a third parent, German folksong. No
one can play through the songs of Schubert and Schumann without noticing how close they often come to the folk idiom, and
Brahms was never tired of proclaiming how folk melodies
delighted and inspired him. It was just because they delighted
and inspired him that he made two collections, one of children's
songs in 1858, the other of a more general nature that he published
in 1894.[1] On these, especially the later one, he lavished immense

[1] Since his death yet other folksong arrangements have been found.
See Appendix B.

care, and always it is the care of the artist, not the musicologist. His one criterion is musical excellence: if a tune pleases him he includes it, though he may know that its authenticity is doubtful. The same exclusive concern with the beauty of the result causes him to harmonize Aeolian tunes in the minor mode, sharpening leading-notes with no more compunction than an editor feels in modernizing Shakespeare's spelling. It has even been suggested that he took still greater liberties, and that two of the best tunes of all, *Schwesterlein* and *In stiller Nacht*, are at least in part his own compositions. This is not the way of the scholar; but as it is a great creative artist we are dealing with should we not be thankful that the scholar's qualms of conscience never troubled him?

Once we grant his premises we are free to appreciate the masterly style in which the task of arrangement has been performed. To make a neat, workmanlike job of the accompaniment to a simple melody remained a joy to him throughout his life. Sometimes he would take folk texts and make new songs of them, fitting them with a tune (as well as an accompaniment) of his own. There are a great number of these songs in the folk manner scattered over his output. If I cite *Vor dem Fenster* (Op. 14 No. 1) and *Dort in den Weiden* (Op. 97 No. 4) it is merely because these may be conveniently compared with the actual folk melodies to the same words that Brahms preserved in his *Deutsche Volkslieder*.

A true folksong is always strophic: each stanza, that is to say, is sung to the same tune. Like Schubert (and unlike Wolf) Brahms never disdained the strophic song, and it is noteworthy that neither composer confines its employment to songs of the folk type. *Der Schmied*[1] (Op. 19 No. 4), with its characteristic

---

[1] I should like to protest against the speed at which so many singers take *Der Schmied*. In spite of the direction *allegro* the big swing of the tune clearly represents the rhythmical muscular effort of the smith as he swings his great hammer. At the pace of some performances one is reminded less of this than of the citizen querulously tapping tin-tacks into the parlour wall.

Brahmsian arpeggio, its big phrases and clanging accompaniment, is no folksong for all its simplicity, still less the impetuous but elaborately organized *Wehe, so willst du mich wieder* (Op. 32 No. 5). Brahms also left a number of dialogue songs in strophic form, but in these both melody and accompaniment are often modified to some extent in one or more of the later stanzas. *Liebestreu* (Op. 3 No. 1) and *Vergebliches Ständchen* (Op. 84 No. 4) are fine examples of this kind of treatment.

It is possible to pursue the strophic song to still loftier regions. Even such masterpieces as *Feldeinsamkeit* (Op. 86 No. 2) and *Sapphische Ode* (Op. 94 No. 4) have a strophic basis. But we are immediately aware that these are richer in content, that they strike deeper than any song we have considered hitherto. Partly it is a difference of scale. Within the broad ground-plan of *Feldeinsamkeit* is room for much that could find no place in a less ample framework. On the one hand a wealth of detail (different in each stanza) must be carefully organized if overcrowding and incoherence are to be avoided. On the other hand a design so large yet so simple fundamentally needs big lines to hold it together. Those immense phrases that tax the singer's breath-control to the uttermost are necessities of the situation. It is a symphonist's song. Only a composer with a symphonist's breadth and a symphonist's instinct for proportion could have achieved it without overstepping the proper bounds of the lyric.

Most of Brahms's highly organized songs are built on a formal basis that is ultimately simple, though obviously it cannot always be strophic. For each poem the fitting shape is found. *Minnelied* (Op. 71 No. 5) falls naturally into a ternary pattern, but its elements are very closely knit and there is no trace of the looseness so often found in association with the conventional aria form. In *Regenlied* and *Nachklang* (Op. 59 Nos. 3 and 4) page after page of music is spun from two tiny pianoforte figures and a vocal refrain that is repeated again and again, but always with a different continuation. Nowhere in Schubert, nowhere in Wolf, do we encounter such ability to proceed easily, lyrically and always eloquently along a predetermined line on a predetermined plan.

- Yet with all this there is a remarkable absence of academic device or ostentatious virtuosity. The canons and inversions that abound in the instrumental and choral works are kept out of the songs. Brahms conceals his art. We may know him for a contrapuntist by the vigour of his basses, the ease and independence of the upper parts, but the tiny snatch of canon that so aptly illustrates the words 'Wir wandelten, wir zwei zusammen,' in Op. 96 No. 2, is altogether exceptional. On the other hand he finds ample scope to indulge his fondness for overlapping phrases. In the dark, passionate *Nicht mehr zu dir zu gehen* (Op. 32 No. 2) the singer's emotion almost stops his speech; the words come in short, broken phrases with rests wherein he struggles for breath, and similar rests in the right hand of the piano part reinforce the impression. But voice and piano do not gasp simultaneously; they are dovetailed together and the labouring procession of crotchets is not checked:

Syncopations and cross-rhythms are common, and their effect is generally excellent. But a curious exception occurs at the end of what is perhaps the best of all his dramatic songs, *Von ewiger Liebe* (Op. 43 No. 1). To strengthen his climax he crosses the established six-eight metre in the voice with three-four in the piano. We may acquit him of deliberate cynicism, but it is a little unfortunate that he chooses the precise moment when the girl proclaims 'Our love shall last for ever' to put voice and piano out of step. The passage is too long to quote in full, but a fragment will illustrate the point:

This raises the whole question of Brahms's attitude to the poetry he set. He is not a poet's composer like Wolf. Poets are inclined to be rather particular about such matters as declamation, and Brahms's declamation is often open to criticism. The first phrase of *Mainacht* (Op. 43 No. 2) forces accents on to the unimportant words 'wann' and 'durch,' and the next phrase begins with an altogether too emphatic 'und':

In *Immer leiser* (Op. 105 No. 2) the first syllable of 'Schlummer' is unduly prolonged simply and solely to make the words fit the tune:

Wolf would never have passed these lapses. He would have maintained that it was the composer's business to find a tune that the words would fit without distortion. Brahms might have replied: 'No! Music has her rights as well as poetry. I dare say I could have found phrases that would fit these verbal sentences exactly, but not such eloquent phrases as I have used; and in lyrical songs like these the melody is the first consideration.' He was a well-educated if mainly self-educated man; he read and appreciated poetry, and if he did not study Wolf's songs at least he was well acquainted with Wagner's operas. Moreover he was the most conscientious of composers. Faulty declamation, where it occurs, is never the result of ignorance and not always of carelessness, but of his attitude towards song, an attitude he thought out thoroughly and maintained consistently. It involves doing occasional violence to the verse, and perhaps that is why he is inclined to be shy of the greatest writers. Goethe and Heine are responsible for a mere handful of his poems, the lion's share going to the insignificant Daumer. Daumer could take it.

Yet it would be a serious mistake to imagine that he was insensitive to the poetry he set. Where in music are we more conscious of the summer noontide heat than in *Feldeinsamkeit*, of the beauty of a summer evening than in *Waldeseinsamkeit* (Op. 85 No. 6)? How convincingly he portrays the slow, uncanny movements of the sleepwalker in *Nachtwandler* (Op. 86 No. 3), the world-weary stoicism of the preacher in the first of the *Vier ernste Gesänge*! Nor is his response limited to such general moods as these. In songs like *Der Tod, das ist die kühle Nacht* (Op. 96 No. 1) or *Mit vierzig Jahren* (Op. 94 No. 1) the music follows every turn of the poet's thought line by line, sometimes word by word. The last-mentioned song, a favourite of Stockhausen's, is unaccountably neglected by modern singers. From the vigorous, thrusting phrase that accompanies the words 'Mit vierzig Jahren ist der Berg erstiegen' to the change to the major key and the glorious broadening that comes with 'Und eh du's denkst, bist du im Port' this is an astonishing example of music's power by its various resources of melody, harmony, modulation and rhythm to reinforce the significance of the poetry that has the good fortune to be linked with it. In the crowning phrase the accent falls, to be sure, on the unimportant word 'bist.' But where is the churl who will cavil at that in such a context?

Not all the songs are of the same high quality. There are some that are dull and more which, while escaping actual dullness, are, let us say, undistinguished. The early sets, too, show a tentativeness that is in marked contrast with the precocious assurance of the first piano works. In spite of an occasional gem it is not till we reach Op. 32 (composed and published in 1864) that we are quite certain of being in the presence of a master. Taking a comprehensive view of the songs as a whole we shall find we have another admission to make: Brahms's range is narrower than either Schubert's or Wolf's. He has written nothing so breathlessly exciting as *Erlkönig*, nothing so subtle, so restrained, yet convincing, as *Nun wandre, Maria*. Most of his songs are lyrics, with love-lyrics predominating. On the other hand, even among these there is plenty of variety. The almost inarticulate passion of *Nicht mehr zu dir zu gehen*, the wild despair of *Der Strom, der neben mir verrauschte* (Op. 32 No. 4), the secret rapture of *Sapphische Ode* are hardly less remote from one another than are all three from the light-hearted flirting of *Vergebliches Ständchen*. Add to these the many fine songs on other themes, such as *O wüsst' ich doch den Weg zurück* (Op. 63 No. 8) with its lament for the lost joys of childhood, or the solemn *Auf dem Kirchhofe* (Op. 105 No. 4), in which, at the poet's bidding, Brahms admits for once an optimistic eschatology — and we must acknowledge that the Brahmsian landscape does not suffer from monotony.

He is a much more spontaneous, more ingenuous fellow, this Brahms of the songs, than the Brahms of the big instrumental works. That formidable 'censor' of his is far less alert. Instrumental music belongs altogether to its composer, the sentiments it expresses are his alone. But in a song he can hide himself behind his poet. It is the poet who sets the mood which the composer is not expected to share save in imagination only. In a song Brahms felt he could relax his control, give rein to the warm, passionate impulses of his nature, all in the interests of the poem and without betraying those inmost secrets of his own being that he guarded so jealously.

So, one may suspect, he argued—and we are the gainers. But the poem is not always such an effective screen as he imagines, and there are occasions when he reveals himself unwittingly. A notable instance is concerned with his fear of death. When, in the sunny *Feldeinsamkeit*, the singer in his remoteness from the everyday world compares himself to one long dead, it is only an idle thought; his mind is not on mortality. Yet what dismal reverberations awake in the composer's soul at that one word 'gestorben'!

In *Mit vierzig Jahren* death is not named at all. But it is implied as the goal to which the downward slope must lead, and that is sufficient to stir the echoes:

Lastly, in the second of the *Four Serious Songs* the same idea is expressed in a phrase whose awful finality can only be fully appreciated in its context:

There is no question here of deliberate cross-references. The three songs quoted belong to different years and are utterly dissimilar in character. Had any one ventured to draw Brahms's attention to the fact that he had said the same thing three times the composer would probably have brought out his stock reply about donkeys. But that will not prevent us from drawing our own conclusions from the remarkable consistency and intensity of his imaginative reactions.

At the last he abandons camouflage and comes out into the open. No one who has listened to the *Four Serious Songs* will doubt that here we have a personal document, a confession of the composer's inmost convictions. The first three songs are all preoccupied with death, which Brahms views from the standpoint of the disillusioned authors of Ecclesiastes and Ecclesiasticus. Never has the philosophy of pessimism found expression at once so moving and so majestic as in this music whose dark splendour marks the summit of his achievement as a song-writer. Yet for all their sombre power he seems to have been conscious of something lacking; their message by itself is too negative. Without paltering with his honesty, had he nothing more positive to tell mankind as he took his leave? Yes, indeed! One other thing he could say: 'Though I speak with the tongues of men and of angels, and have not love [1] . . .' The first part of the song does not perhaps rise to the full height of the words. Only when we reach 'For now we see through a glass darkly' does the music begin to glow. How many of these smooth *adagio* melodies has Brahms composed, yet still the spell has power! But the climax is to come: 'And now abideth these three . . .' Putting forth his full strength he writes perhaps the grandest phrase in all his vocal music, a superb arch spanning nearly two octaves:

Nun___ a-ber blei - bet__ Glau - be, Hoff - nung,

Lie - - - be, die - se drei,___

Faith he lacked, Hope had deserted him, but to the third of St. Paul's anchors he held fast, and so holding could depart with a smile and a benediction.

[1] Whatever the relative merits of the two English translations of ἀγάπη the German word is 'Liebe,' which does *not* mean 'charity.'

## §2. DUETS AND QUARTETS

Over the duets for soprano and contralto there is no need to
linger. They rarely seek to do more than please and none of them
compares in importance with the more significant of the solo
songs. Yet where the required voices and a pianist are gathered
together they will find satisfaction in the rich colours and cunning
part-writing of *Phänomen* (Op. 61 No. 3), the far-ranging modulation in the middle section of *Am Strande* (Op. 66 No. 3), and there
is a plaintive charm about the two little songs called *Klänge*
(Op. 66 Nos. 1 and 2), the second of which has the same melody
as the slow movement of the F♯ minor piano Sonata.

The four duets for contralto and baritone (Op. 28) and the
*Ballads and Romances* (Op. 75) for various combinations of voices
are largely in dialogue form, though there are passages in all of
them where the voices combine, and they cannot therefore be
performed (like *Vergebliches Ständchen*) by a single singer. In the
earlier set *Es rauscht das Wasser* (No. 3) makes a graceful, attractive
song, and in the later the uncanny *Walpurgisnacht* (No. 4), for two
sopranos, will always make its effect. It is, however, rather over-
shadowed by the dark, powerful *Edward* (No. 1) for contralto and
tenor. Pianists will recollect that Brahms had been interested in
this grim poem as far back as the first of the *Ballades*, Op. 10. His
setting here is appropriately tragic and stormy, but he handicaps
himself cruelly by composing it in an almost unbroken series of
balanced four-bar phrases. Loewe's freer treatment of the same
poem is more dramatic and makes a deeper impression. The
fact is that Brahms's style is too incorrigibly lyrical for him to appear
at his best in an undertaking of this sort.

For the quartets (with piano accompaniment) a lyrical style is
all that is required. *Wechsellied zum Tanze* (Op. 31 No. 1) is a
foretaste of what was to come. It consists of an alternation of
minuet (contralto and bass) and waltz (soprano and tenor), the
four voices only combining for the final section. *Der Gang zum
Liebchen* (Op. 31 No. 3) avows its *Ländler* origin still more openly,

being no more than a somewhat elaborated arrangement of the four-hand waltz, Op. 39 No. 5. Schubert is the model for these pieces and for the *Liebeslieder* Waltzes (Op. 52) and *Neue Liebes-lieder* (Op. 65) that were to follow. The Hamburg bear cannot quite achieve the light-foot Viennese gaiety that was Schubert's birthright, but he dances with unexpected zeal and geniality none the less. Every number (except the very last of the *Neue Liebeslieder*) is in waltz time, and the piano part, laid out for four hands, is of unusual importance.

Different in mood and metre (they are all in two-four), but similar in lightness of touch and directness of appeal are the *Zigeunerlieder*, which comprise the whole of Op. 103 and Nos. 3–6 of Op. 112. Though some of them sound more German than gypsy, others are more convincing, dainty and passionate by turns and always capricious.

Singers who are prepared to enjoy themselves lightheartedly will find delight in all these groups of quartets. For graver moods Brahms does not serve them so well. *Sehnsucht* and *Nächtens* (from Op. 112), especially *Nächtens* with its five-four metre, are successful pieces of tone-painting, but the Op. 64 and Op. 92 quartets, though mellifluous, are not particularly interesting. Perhaps the best of them is *Warum?* (Op. 92 No. 4), even if the promise of its dramatic opening is not quite fulfilled in the six-eight movement that follows.

# CHAPTER XI

## CHORAL MUSIC

THERE is something of the tadpole about Brahms's choral works. For the head we have the Requiem, by far the best, by far the most popular of them all. After this the tadpole dwindles rapidly: whatever the merits of the *Alto Rhapsody* and the *Song of Destiny* they are not to be compared with the Requiem, nor are they nearly so frequently performed. The *Song of the Fates* is heard even more seldom and the remaining five pieces for chorus and orchestra are practically unknown to the concert-going public. Of the part-songs, motets and so on an occasional number may stray into a programme now and again, and that is about all. Even the scores of some of these are hard to come by in these difficult days.

To find a lot of neglected music in the output of an acknowledged master is nothing unusual, nor in the case of Brahms's choral works is the neglect at all incomprehensible, for it must be admitted that his genius burns more fitfully here than anywhere else. Amid a good deal that is dull or insignificant it is easy to overlook the exceptional piece that is alive all through.

## §1. SONGS FOR FEMALE VOICES

It is disappointing to find a large proportion of this inferior music among the songs composed for female voices. Nearly all these were written for the Detmold choir or the Hamburg Ladies' Choir.[1] Remembering the delight the young Johannes took in these institutions one expects to see some of it reflected in the music. A trace may in fact be found in the fresh and innocent

[1] Opp. 37 and 44 were not published till 1866, but there is reason to believe that some, at any rate, of these songs were sung by the Hamburg Ladies' Choir before its dissolution. The same is true of at least six of the Canons in Op. 113, despite their high opus number.

*Ave Maria*, Op. 12, though the style is tentative and the orchestration clumsy. But the songs with accompaniment for two horns and harp (Op. 17) do not come up to expectations; in the instrumental writing Brahms fails to take full advantage of his opportunities, and much of the music is rather dull, though an exception must be made in favour of the *Song from Fingal* which makes an effective dirge. The songs of Op. 44 are conventionally charming, but very slight, and the Canons of Op. 113 have a limited aesthetic value, though they are exceedingly ingenious and must be good fun to sing. Of the two sacred works (other than the *Ave Maria*) the setting of the *Thirteenth Psalm* (Op. 27) is curiously lifeless and uninteresting, and the three songs to Latin texts (Op. 37) sound just what they are, skilful exercises in canon, with very few pretensions to other qualities.

## §2. SONGS FOR MALE VOICES

The single set of songs for male voices (Op. 41) is sufficiently described by its title, *Soldiers' Songs*. Diatonic for the most part, and straightforward in design and treatment, these compositions show more vigour and character than most of the works for female voices.

## §3. PARTSONGS FOR MIXED VOICES

Under this heading are found songs of very varying merit. There is a naïve, old-fashioned quality about the *Sieben Marienlieder* (Op. 22) that makes them rather attractive, but they are too slight to be taken very seriously. Not much more substantial, though not without charm, are Opp. 62 (Seven Songs for unaccompanied chorus) and 93A (Six Partsongs for chorus). Only here and there does a number such as the six-part *All' meine Herzgedanken* in Op. 62 or *Fahr wohl* in the later set make a really definite impression. *Fahr wohl*, which was sung at the composer's funeral, is a profoundly moving piece of music for all its simplicity. The *Tafellied* (Op. 93B) is longer than any of these and has an independent piano accompaniment, but does not aspire to be more than a good, hearty piece of Teutonic rollicking.

Rather more solid fare is provided by the six-part unaccompanied songs of Op. 42. *Vineta*, the second one, is a fine, richly coloured bit of work, and the third number, *Darthula's Burial Song*, contains impressive music. Both of these ought to be better known. But it is not till we reach the Five Partsongs, Op. 104, that we encounter the high imagination of the best of the solo songs. The first of the two six-part compositions entitled *Nachtwache* and the four-part *Im Herbst* are delicately sensitive in expression and masterly in technique. But most of us will agree with Elisabeth von Herzogenberg in giving first place to the second *Nachtwache*, a noble song wherein the solemn question 'Do they rest?' is answered by the assurance, 'They rest,' to music 'warm with the glow of sunset and the sound of bugles.'[1]

The Fourteen German Folksongs that Brahms published in 1864 are quite independent of the Forty-nine German Folksongs of 1894, although it is true that a few tunes appear in both collections. This earlier set consists entirely of four-part songs, some of them simple harmonizations of folk melodies, others much more elaborate. The composer obviously enjoyed building up these unsophisticated ditties into complex but never ponderous structures, with points of imitation and free, flowing counterpoint. Choral conductors on the look-out for lively, attractive and musicianly songs that are by no means familiar may be recommended to search among these pieces. Since Brahms's death twelve more of them have come to light and are included in the Breitkopf & Härtel collection of the complete works, edited by Eusebius Mandyczewski.

### §4. Motets, etc.

With the three great sets of Motets (Opp. 29, 74 and 110), to which we may add the *Sacred Song* with organ accompaniment

[1] See Elisabeth's letter to Brahms of 28th October 1888 for her admirable comments on the whole of Op. 104.

(Op. 30), we leave the comfortable, warmly coloured valley of the partsongs for a bleak upland of austere living and high thinking. Death is our constant companion; again and again we are invited to contemplate the vanity of life, the transitory nature of happiness. To a man with Brahms's background these subjects and the choral medium inevitably suggest Bach, the Bach of the motets and chorale preludes. Like Bach he is fond of taking a chorale melody as his basis, sometimes for the whole motet (as in Op. 29 No. 1 and Op. 74 No. 2), sometimes for a single movement (Op. 74 No. 1); in *Wenn wir in höchsten Nöten sind* (Op. 110 No. 3) he ignores altogether the tune in the major key with which Bach has made us familiar, substitutes a much more angular, but still chorale-like phrase in the minor and builds a great part of his motet from that one phrase alone. Not all the motets contain chorales, and the design varies with each separate work. But with all their differences one quality is found in every one of them: a prodigious command of contrapuntal resource. Here, as nowhere else, Brahms's powers of combination are displayed in all their amplitude. He will treat a melody antiphonally (Op. 110 No. 3), superimpose it on a fugue that is itself derived from the tune it is accompanying (Op. 29 No. 1), or weave in a canon by inversion (fourth verse of Op. 74 No. 2). Even an apparently straightforward piece of writing like the majestic opening of Op. 29 No. 2 turns out to conceal a canon by augmentation, and Op. 74 No. 2 ends with an 'Amen' containing a canon four in one, followed by another four in two, both by inversion.

Choirs that know how to negotiate awkward corners will find plenty to interest them in this contrapuntal legerdemain. Its effect on the listener can be gauged with less certainty and will depend on the personal equation. If he can enjoy Bach's 'Art of Fugue' he will probably enjoy Brahms's motets. No composer can submit to a technical discipline so severe as this without some shackling of the imagination, and there are times when the unrelenting sternness of the music declines into aridity. Another man might have compromised, relaxed the discipline and avoided the aridity. Brahms is too high-minded for that; he will not disfigure these essays in the sublime by paltering with his lofty theme, and his fault is that of Browning's grammarian who, 'aiming at a million, misses a unit.' We may turn from the motets if we will, but in so doing we shall miss the fullest expression of his most secret thoughts that Brahms has managed to utter. The communication of the mysteries of the spirit can never be easy.

Where he has less solemn matter to discuss he changes his style entirely. Handel, not Bach, is the model for the much more genial *Fest und Gedenksprüche* (eight parts, *a cappella*, Op. 109) that celebrated his reconciliation with Hamburg in 1889. This is broad, vigorous music of a splendid sonority, breathing a less rarefied air than the motets.

### §5. WORKS FOR CHORUS AND ORCHESTRA

The earliest of the choral works with orchestra, the *Ave Maria*, Op. 12, has been noticed among the pieces for female voices. In the next one, the *Funeral Hymn*, Op. 13, the young man of twenty-five fights the first round of his long wrestling match with the Angel of Death. Scored for four-part chorus and an orchestra of wind only, the hymn shows obvious signs of youth, but is highly effective for all that. The hand that penned the opening strain:

Nun lasst uns den Leib be - gra - ben

is recognizably the same as that which was to write this in the *Four Serious Songs*:

Denn es ge - het dem Men - schen wie dem Vieh.

For his Requiem (Op. 45) the composer took his words from Luther's Bible, selecting the texts himself with great care. His work has no relation whatever to the canonical Office of the Dead. No prayer is offered for the departed. What use is prayer to one who has ceased to be? The name of Christ is avoided.[1] Brahms has only one object, the consolation of the living. 'Blessed are they that mourn, for they shall be comforted' is the message of the first chorus, which is supported by an orchestra from which the bright tones of clarinets, trumpets and violins have been wholly excluded. The second movement is one of the grandest of the composer's inspirations, a funeral march in three-time to the words 'Behold, all flesh is as grass':

He was always happiest, said his friends, when he could sing 'My joy is in the grave,' and the quip finds some justification here, for the end of the movement describing the 'joy everlasting' of the redeemed does not reach the level of the march. 'Lord, make me to know the measure of my days' declaims the baritone soloist at the beginning of the third movement. Solo and chorus are used antiphonally in music of steadily increasing intensity till the culmination is reached with the fugue (on a tonic pedal throughout): 'But the righteous souls are in the hand of God.' I confess I find this fugue unconvincing: its subject seems to have been chosen more for its contrapuntal implications than its emotional significance. After it comes an interlude, 'How lovely is thy dwelling-place,' wherein Brahms achieves a Mendelssohnian sweetness without ever sinking into Mendelssohnian sentimentality.

[1] It is a pity that in at least one English translation the words 'bis auf die Zukunft des Herrn' are rendered 'unto the coming of the Christ.'

We must be grateful for the happy afterthought that gave us the soprano solo. Here at last is the genuine ray from on high. 'Yea, I will comfort you,' sings the soprano, 'as one whom his own mother comforteth,' and the chorus echoes the words to strains wherein sorrow melts in sheer lyric loveliness. But the spirit must be purged before it can gain final tranquillity. At the beginning of the sixth number the chorus is groping in uneasy darkness: 'Here on earth have we no continuing place.' Out of the gloom comes the solemn call of the baritone solo: 'Lo, I unfold unto you a mystery.' In the finest dramatic pages Brahms ever wrote humanity awaits the revelation with growing anxiety. Soft, grave chords on trombones [1] announce the trumpet of doom; there is a wild outburst of violins; to great shouts of triumph from chorus and orchestra death is swallowed up in victory and the whole body of performers launches out into a splendid, exultant fugue: 'Worthy art Thou to be praised, Lord of honour and might.' It is the paean of release. After it the mourner can return to his private griefs with his soul at peace, and the last movement recalls the first. But (a significant point) there is no longer a reason for silencing the violins.

As the years went on Brahms learnt to subtilize his harmony and orchestration beyond anything found in the Requiem. But he never wrote another vocal work of equal breadth, nor one so consistently inspired as this masterpiece of his early maturity.

Of the four choral compositions that he completed during the two years following the Requiem two have fallen by the wayside. We need not regret the dramatic Cantata *Rinaldo* (Op. 50); it moves on feet of lead and never approaches the effectiveness of the sixth movement of the Requiem. But artistically it is a pity that the Prussian victories of 1870 are not among those that modern audiences care to celebrate, for the eight-part *Triumphlied* (Song of Triumph, Op. 55) is in the composer's most sonorous,

[1] In the German the last trumpet is a last trombone (*Posaune*). I take this opportunity to remark on the many beautiful passages for *piano* trombones, nearly all of them dramatic, in the *Requiem*.

Handelian vein. 'Not difficult, only *forte*,' was his own laconic description.

The *Rhapsody* (Op. 53) for contralto, male chorus and orchestra is a most interesting work. In harmony and orchestration its first part is not quite like anything else in Brahms. Here the solo contralto describes the unhappy recluse who hated mankind in a strangely expressive song that oscillates between six-four and three-two, and contains phrases with such un-Brahmsian contours as this:

Aus___ der Fül - le der Lie · · · ·
- - - be___ trank?

With the entry of the male chorus the style becomes more conventional, though the solo part never altogether loses its individual quality.

The *Schicksalslied* (Song of Destiny, Op. 54), on the other hand, is entirely typical of its author. It presents us, however, with an odd problem in psychology. A serene prelude of considerable length and in the key of E♭ major introduces the first section of Hölderlin's poem wherein the felicity of the gods on their remote Olympus is described in a chorus full of those sleek, *legato* phrases that Brahms knew so well how to write. Then comes an abrupt change. Double-bowed string passages, in a stormy C minor reminiscent of the apocalyptic vision in the Requiem, bring the turmoil of earth, where miserable humanity is doomed to wander restlessly till at last it is hurled into the abyss. Beyond this Hölderlin says nothing; he presents his contrast, but draws no conclusion. Brahms, however, is not satisfied with so stark an ending: he slides from C minor into C major, and in this bright tonality repeats the whole of his serene, celestial prelude. Is he merely following an inclination to round off his work on a

conventional ternary pattern? Is he blind to the appalling in-
appropriateness of such an epilogue to such a poem? He is not
generally so insensitive. Besides, if that were all, why not write
the epilogue in E♭, the key of the prelude? But whatever its
weaknesses, this explanation is preferable to that of the senti-
mentalists who hold that Brahms is asserting against Hölderlin
that after all 'God's in his heaven, all's right with the world.'
If you can believe that of the composer of the Requiem and the
*Four Serious Songs* you can believe anything. A third possibility
is that the epilogue is trying to tell us that the fate of mankind is
altogether indifferent to the gods. They feast on, uncaring. That
has at least the merit of harmonizing with views expressed by the
composer elsewhere. But the enigma is not one that can be
solved with certainty. For once Brahms has failed to make
himself clear.

*Nänie* (Op. 82) was written in memory of his friend Anselm
Feuerbach, the painter. 'Even the beautiful must die. Yet to
be a song of lament in the mouth of a friend is glorious.' Taking
his cue from this last sentiment Brahms composes a rich, melodious threnody, most grateful to sing. The music deserves something better than the almost complete oblivion into which it has
fallen.[1] Its companion piece, the *Gesang der Parzen* (Song of the
Fates, Op. 89), has fared somewhat better, though not much.
'In fear of the gods shall ye dwell, sons of men' is the burden of
Goethe's words, which are set for a very full orchestra and a six-
part choir. By writing two alto and two bass parts and only one
soprano and one tenor Brahms achieves a characteristically dark
quality.[2] The music is highly concentrated, and there is no

[1] It is noteworthy that at the words 'The Highest dies! The Beautiful fades' the orchestra falls into the same formula of hollow descending
octaves that is used for death in the solo songs. See p. 153.

[2] I ought to observe that this disposition of voices, though peculiarly
appropriate to the *Song of the Fates*, is often used by Brahms elsewhere.
See, for instance, the six-part songs, Op. 62. He had a temperamental
inclination towards dark, rich colours.

denying the power of this bitterest of his arraignments of the unpitying heavens. In place of the serene conclusion of the *Song of Destiny,* the *Song of the Fates* ends with a shiver, the orchestra wrenching the harmony from F♯ minor into D minor (the tonic) at the last possible moment, the chorus falling in bare octaves into the silence of despair. It is not a comfortable cadence, but this is not a comfortable poem—nor was Brahms in this mood a very comfortable person.

# CHAPTER XII

## BRAHMS TO-DAY

'THAT he stands beside Bach and Beethoven is hardly any more a matter for controversy. . . . When music attains to fuller knowledge and nobler practice, it will grant him a due place among its foremost leaders, and to us who honour him as a monarch, will succeed a generation which reverences him as a hero.'

Thus wrote Sir Henry Hadow many years ago. It has not turned out quite like that. Brahms's equality with Bach and Beethoven is by no means universally accepted to-day, nor is 'hero' quite the word we should select for him. But then who is to say whether music has attained 'to fuller knowledge and nobler practice'? Time never answers all questions and the debate on Brahms is still very much alive, though the ground has shifted a good deal since the appearance of the famous manifesto against the neo-German school. That controversy at any rate is dead, and Wagnerians and 'Brahmins' are no longer divided into hostile camps. Both these masters claimed Beethoven as the source of their art and both, as we can see now, were right. What both failed to realize was that the waters of that copious spring could flow in diverse directions to fertilize here the dramatic art of a Wagner, there the symphonic art of a Brahms. To us the tragedy is that Brahms and Wagner should have quarrelled, for they had much in common: artistic integrity, a love and understanding of Beethoven that no composer of their day could rival, a desire and capacity to create on the grand scale, together with the logical, critical faculty essential to such creation. Like Balen and Balan in the old tale they were a pair of brothers doomed not to recognize one another, and to spend in sterile warfare the energies that would have made them resistless in combination. To-day we can admire the music of both without feeling guilty of treachery to either; we can even concede the virtues of Liszt without faltering in our homage to Brahms. In the broad nineteenth-century landscape there was room for all these things.

We can see from our vantage-point of 1966 that Schumann was wrong: Brahms was not to be the prophet of a new age. He is no founder of a new dynasty, not even an intermediate name in a long continuous line, but the very last of the classical Caesars. With all his popularity, all his prestige, he occupied a singularly isolated position during his last years. No composer of anything like his calibre was working on lines that approximated to his; [1] no one harmonized as he did, orchestrated as he did; no significant symphonies or quartets were written on the dignified classical plan of his symphonies and chamber music. It was from Liszt and from Wagner that the young men drew their inspiration, the young men who would have the field to themselves in Germany when he was gone—Strauss, Wolf, Mahler and the rest. The still more youthful Schoenberg, who was beginning to compose in the nineties, owes in his early works much to Wagner, something perhaps to Schubert, nothing to Brahms. Nor has a later generation reversed the verdict. After all the vast changes European music has undergone in the last fifty years the influence of Wagner and Liszt is still easily discernible. But where is the influence of Brahms? It is a strange phenomenon. Here is a master who not only gained universal recognition, but whose reputation seemed to be based on the solidest possible foundation. Since his death he has not been forgotten. His music is played everywhere, respected everywhere, loved everywhere—only somehow nobody does anything about it.

As regards England a partial exception must be made. Unlike Mendelssohn, Brahms steadfastly refused to visit this country, and it might have been supposed that his style was too massive, too German for the British public, that he was too scornful of the airs and graces by which that public set store in the reign of Queen Victoria, to find much favour. But he was introduced to us by

[1] There were Max Reger and Rheinberger. But few would put these among the giants.

those two popular visitors, Joachim and Clara Schumann, and he never lacked advocates, both British and foreign, to press his claims. His friend, George Henschel, settled in England in 1885, and was active both as singer and conductor in Brahms's interests. Perhaps British Toryism found something substantial and reliable in this music that was congenial. Anyhow it made slow but quite steady progress. Misunderstandings naturally arose at first. Florence May tells of a controversy that raged as to whether Brahms had ever been in England. One old gentleman was very positive: of course Brahms had been in England! He himself had often seen him and heard him sing *The Death of Nelson*. The old gentleman was confusing him with John Braham, the singer, who died in 1856. But the time was soon to come when Braham was forgotten and Brahms's name was known to all. The enthusiasm of C. V. Stanford and Hubert Parry helped very greatly in building up his reputation. Both these composers owe more to Brahms than does any comparable foreign composer, and as they came more and more into prominence they carried him along with them. Their influence was very great, especially in the educational field, and it is no doubt largely due to them that in many present-day English textbooks on harmony Brahms is the last composer whose music is systematically analysed, later writers being rather perfunctorily covered in a final chapter on 'modern developments.'

Such was the state of affairs in the period immediately preceding the First World War. Everywhere Brahms was played and sung, his devotees were ardent and numerous. In fact they rather overdid it, and they have only themselves to thank if there has been something of a reaction since. They claimed too much for their hero, with the result that now he is sometimes accorded too little. 'Debunking' Brahms has become almost as fashionable as 'debunking' Mendelssohn was forty years ago, and for the same reason. Mendelssohn, the idol of nineteenth-century England, fell in two or three decades from the summit of Olympus to the depths of Tartarus. Only now are we beginning to appre-

170

ciate how little he deserved either situation. It may be that Brahms will have to undergo a similar process before a criticism can be written that is entirely unprejudiced.

While awaiting that final judgment we may observe that for present-day musicians he is mainly an instrumental composer; the vocal works, though hardly less in bulk, do not attract so much attention. That much of the choral music has disappeared into limbo need not distress us; reasons for that have been advanced in the previous chapter, reasons inherent in the compositions themselves—though we may regret that a few pieces of value have somehow got on to the refuse-heap with their less worthy brethren.

At first sight the neglect of the solo songs is harder to account for. We may admit that they are not all of equal merit, and yet feel that they are not adequately represented by the handful of examples that appear again and again in our concert programmes to the exclusion of all the rest. A little consideration, however, will do much to dispose of the difficulty. Let us take note, to begin with, that Brahms has not been the only sufferer; none of the 'big four' has gone unscathed. The fact is that they have all been rather too generous. Brahms has left some two hundred songs, Schumann about the same number, Wolf rather more, Schubert over six hundred. No appetite can possibly absorb such a Gargantuan feast as that. Even in the great days at the end of the nineteenth century and the beginning of the twentieth, when the idiom was still more or less contemporary, and it was treason to dispute the supremacy of the *Lied* over every other kind of song, a process of elimination was quietly at work weeding out the weaker songs of Brahms and Wolf; those of Schubert and Schumann had gone already. The years rolled by, the romantic attitude ceased to be fashionable; one by one the great practitioners of the *Lied* departed, and with the passing of each the tradition was weakened. Then (in England) it suddenly sustained a grievous blow from without, a blow against which there was no protection: during the war of 1914–18 the German language was virtually prohibited. A similar prohibition during the years

1939–45 was only a little less effective. The damage done by these two compulsory breaks in continuity has been immense. Meanwhile—and partly as a result of the decline of the *Lied*, which left room for other things—English singers were finding new worlds to conquer, exploring folksong or Dowland, Mus-sorgsky or Debussy, or assisting with lively interest the modern renaissance of English song. To-day *Lieder* are still to be heard in our concert halls, but they occupy only a single province in the singer's realm. The repertory has shrunk, the general standard of performance fallen. Brahms's range is narrower than Schu-bert's or Wolf's, and it may be that his songs have suffered more drastically than theirs from the winnowing of time. It would be interesting to know how many English singers at this moment have a working knowledge of, say, forty of them—a fifth of the whole. The *Lied* was perhaps the most typical musical product of the romantic revival. It may conceivably prove the most ephemeral.[1]

Among the instrumental works, on the other hand, the casualty list has proved astonishingly small. One or two of the youthful piano works have dropped out, the orchestral Serenades are not often heard, but there is no sign whatever of the symphonies, the concertos, the chamber music or the intermezzi losing their hold on the public. Are all these things really sterile, or is it merely that they germinate very slowly? It was a long time before Bach's music had much influence on the general development of the art. For more than half a century after his death musical evolution was on lines that made his contribution for the time being irrele-vant. When at length he came into his own with the romantic revival the lessons learnt from him were used for purposes of which he never dreamt; but that did not prevent him from

---

[1] I have confined my remarks on this topic to England. Obviously in the German-speaking countries the course of events has been different, but my impression is that it has led to a somewhat similar result so far as the *Lied* is concerned.

becoming (with Beethoven) the most fructifying influence in nineteenth-century music.

It may turn out that way with Brahms, even if we admit, as most of us do, that he is a lesser man than Bach. At present he stands, as Bach stood, at the end of a line. Composers have turned to other things, and though they will listen to Brahms and honour him, they do not find that he can help them much with their own problems. Perhaps he has only to wait, perhaps another turn of the wheel will produce a situation in which he can once more be of service, when musicians will find in him the inspiration for some new development, the nature of which is altogether hidden from us. Or perhaps the wheel will never turn that way. There is even the possibility that Bach, Beethoven and Brahms will go down together in a wreck of our civilization. What then? Surely this: if a man has worked hard and wrought valiantly, if he has persevered unswerving in pursuit of a noble ideal, if he has given delight and courage to thousands—and Brahms has done all these things—then he needs no further justification. He has deserved his place in the sun. The world is sweeter for his sojourn in it.

# APPENDICES

## APPENDIX A

### CALENDAR

*(Figures in brackets denote the age reached by the person mentioned during the year in question.)*

| Year | Age | Life | Contemporary Musicians |
|------|-----|------|------------------------|
| 1833 | | Johannes Brahms born May 7, in Hamburg, son of Johann Jakob Brahms (27), double bass player. | Auber aged 51; Balfe 25; Bellini 32; Berlioz 30; Bishop 47; Boieldieu 58; Bruckner 9; Cherubini 73; Chopin 23; Cornelius 9; Dargomijsky 20; Donizetti 36; Field 51; Franck 11; Franz 18; Gade 16; Glinka 30; Goldmark 3; Gounod 15; Halévy 34; Kirchner 10; Lalo 10; Liszt 22; Loewe 37; Lortzing 30; Marschner 38; Mendelssohn 24; Mercadante 38; Meyerbeer 42; Nicolai 23; Offenbach 14; Paer 62; Raff 11; Rossini 41; Schumann 23; Smetana 9; Spohr 49; Spontini 59; Strauss (J. ii) 8; Verdi 20; Wagner 20. Boieldieu (59) dies, Oct. 8; Borodin born, Oct. 31/Nov. 12. |
| 1835 | 2 | Birth of brother, Friedrich (Fritz) Brahms, March 26. | Bellini (34) dies, Sept. 24; Cui born, Jan. 6/18; Draeseke born, Oct. 7; Saint-Saëns born, Oct. 9. |
| 1836 | 3 | | Delibes born, Feb. 21. |
| 1837 | 4 | | Balakirev born, Jan. 11 (N.S.); Field (55) dies, Jan. 11. |

| Year | Age | Life | Contemporary Musicians |
|------|-----|------|------------------------|
| 1838 | 5 | | Bizet born, Oct. 25; Bruch born, Jan. 6. |
| 1839 | 6 | Learns the elements of music from his father (33). | Mussorgsky born, March 9/21; Paer (68) dies, May 3; Rheinberger born, March 17. |
| 1840 | 7 | Tuition under his father (34) continues, with the object of making him an orchestral player. Takes piano lessons from Cossel (28). | Götz born, Dec. 17; Stainer born, June 6; Svendsen born, Sept. 3; Tchaikovsky born, April 25/May 7. |
| 1841 | 8 | | Chabrier born, Jan. 18; Dvořák born, Sept. 8; Pedrell born, Feb. 19. |
| 1842 | 9 | Makes rapid progress at the piano. | Boito born, Feb. 24; Cherubini (82) dies, March 15; Massenet born, May 12; Sullivan born May 13. |
| 1843 | 10 | Cossel (30) recommends him to Marxsen (37), who gives him piano lessons. Plays at a private subscription concert for funds for his future education. | Grieg born, June 15; Herzogenberg born, June 10; Sgambati born, May 28. |
| 1844 | 11 | Cossel (31) opposes a suggestion that he should be taken on tour as a prodigy. | Rimsky-Korsakov born, March 6/18. |
| 1845 | 12 | Becomes now entirely the pupil of Marxsen (39) and begins to improvise compositions at the piano. | Fauré born, May 13. |
| 1846 | 13 | Marxsen (40) begins to teach him theory. He earns some money by playing at humble places of entertainment. | Brüll born, Nov. 7. |
| 1847 | 14 | His health is impaired by his playing at sailors' taverns and dancing saloons at night. | Mackenzie born, Aug. 22; Mendelssohn (38) dies, Nov. 4. |

| *Year* | *Age* | *Life* | *Contemporary Musicians* |
|---|---|---|---|
| | | Giesemann, a music lover, invites him to spend a long holiday at Winsen-an-der-Luhe, where he composes *A B C* and *Postilions Morgenlied* for male voice choir. | |
| 1848 | 15 | Summer again spent at Winsen, where he conducts a small male voice choir. Back at Hamburg, he gives his first concert on his own account, Sept. 21. | Donizetti (51) dies, April 8; Duparc born, Jan. 21; Parry born, Feb. 27. |
| 1849 | 16 | Gives a concert, April 14, at which he plays his own *Fantasia on a Favourite Waltz*. Having failed to begin a satisfactory career, he gives cheap lessons, continues to play at dancing saloons and arranges popular music for the piano. | Chopin (40) dies, Oct. 17; Nicolai (39) dies, May 11. |
| 1850 | 17 | Many songs composed. Meeting with Reményi (20), who makes him acquainted with Hungarian national dances. | |
| 1851 | 18 | Lessons and hack work continued. Scherzo, E♭ minor for piano (Op. 4), composed. | d'Indy born, March 27; Lortzing (48) dies, Jan. 21; Spontini (77) dies, Jan. 14. |
| 1852 | 19 | Piano Sonata, F♯ minor (Op. 2). | Stanford born, Sept. 30. |
| 1853 | 20 | Piano Sonata, C major (Op. 1). Concert tour with Reményi (23), April. Meeting with Joachim (22) at Hanover, who engages them to play at the court of | |

| Year | Age | Life | Contemporary Musicians |
|------|-----|------|------------------------|
| | | Hanover and sends them with an introduction to Liszt (42) at Weimar. B. meets Cornelius (29) and Raff (31) there. Walking tour through the Rhineland, and composition of piano Sonata, F minor (Op. 5), begun. Meeting with Hiller (42) and Reinecke (29) at Cologne and with Schumann (43) at Düsseldorf. Great friendship with him and Clara Schumann (34). Violin and piano Sonata for Joachim written jointly with Schumann and Dietrich (24), Oct. Schumann writes an enthusiastic article on B. in the *Neue Zeitschrift für Musik*, Oct. 28, and sends him with recommendations to Leipzig, where he finds two publishers, meets Berlioz (50) and plays two of his works at a concert, Dec. 17. | |
| 1854 | 21 | Piano Trio, B major (Op. 8), Feb. B. hastens to Düsseldorf on hearing of Schumann's (44) mental breakdown and attempt at suicide, early March, and assists Clara Schumann (35). Variations on a theme of Schumann, for piano (Op. 9), June. Later, Ballades for piano (Op. 10). Symphony | Humperdinck born, Sept. 1; Janáček born, July 4. |

| *Year* | *Age* | *Life* | *Contemporary Musicians* |
|---|---|---|---|
| | | in D minor begun, but abandoned and converted into a Sonata for two pianos. | |
| 1855 | 22 | Lives and teaches at Düsseldorf, but spends a good deal of time on concert tours. | Bishop (69) dies, April 30; Chausson born, Jan. 21; Liadov born, April 29/ May 11. |
| 1856 | 23 | Goes to live at Bonn, to be near the dying Schumann (46), spring. Meeting with Klaus Groth (37). Two concerts given with Stockhausen (30) at Cologne and Bonn, May. B. remains near Clara Schumann (37) after her husband's death. | Martucci born, Jan. 1; Schumann (46) dies, July 29; Sinding born, Jan. 11; Taneiev born, Nov. 13/25. |
| 1857 | 24 | Visit to the court of Lippe-Detmold, where he teaches the piano to the Princess Friederike and conducts the choral society, Sept.-Dec. Folksongs arranged for the choir. | Elgar born, June 2; Glinka (54) dies, Feb. 15. |
| 1858 | 25 | Summer spent at Göttingen. 14 Folksongs for Children arranged for Clara Schumann's (39) children. Piano Concerto, D minor (Op. 15), rehearsed by Joachim (27) at Hanover, Oct. Duties at Detmold resumed, autumn, and *Ave Maria* for female voices (Op. 12) written there. | Leoncavallo born, March 8; Puccini born, June 22; Smyth (Ethel) born, April 23. |
| 1859 | 26 | D minor piano Concerto performed by B. at Hanover and Leipzig, Jan. 22 and 27. | Spohr (75) dies, Oct. 22. |

| Year | Age | Life | Contemporary Musicians |
|------|-----|------|------------------------|
| | | It is unsuccessful, especially in Leipzig, but favourably received in Hamburg, March 24. First performance of Serenade for small orchestra, D major (Op. 11), March 28. B. is appointed conductor of a ladies' choir at Hamburg, which performs the *Marienlieder* (Op. 22) and the 13th Psalm (Op. 27), Sept. 19. Duties at Detmold again resumed, autumn. Piano Quartet, G minor (Op. 25, 1st version), and Serenade for small orchestra, A major (Op. 16), composed there. | |
| 1860 | 27 | Leaves Detmold, Jan., and does not renew his engagement. Takes part in a press manifesto against the 'New German' school headed by Liszt (49), which is inadvertently published too soon with only four signatures, May. Sextet for strings, B♭ major (Op. 18), finished, autumn. Variations on an Original Theme for piano (Op. 21 No. 1) produced by Clara Schumann (41) in Leipzig, Dec. 8. | Albéniz born, May 29; Mahler born, July 7; Wolf born, March 13. |
| 1861 | 28 | Lives at Hamburg and makes frequent public appearances. Piano Quartet, G minor (Op. 25), revised | MacDowell born, Dec. 18; Marschner (66) dies, Dec. 14. |

| Year | Age | Life | Contemporary Musicians |
|------|-----|------|------------------------|
| | | and that in A major (Op. 26) begun. Variations on a theme by Handel for piano (Op. 24). | |
| 1862 | 29 | Composition of string Quintet, F minor (later Sonata for 2 pianos and piano Quintet), summer. First visit to Vienna, where he is cordially received, Sept. Stockhausen (36) being appointed conductor of the Philharmonic concerts and the *Singakademie* in Hamburg, B. is inclined to turn | Debussy born, Aug. 22; Delius born, Jan. 29; Halévy (62) dies, March 17. |
| 1862 | 29 | his back on his native city. He goes on a tour, however, until after Christmas. Publication of Partsongs for female voices with two horns and harp (Op. 17), also Opp. 18, 19, 22 and 24. | |
| 1863 | 30 | In Vienna again, B. gives a concert to introduce his songs to the Austrian public, Jan. 6. With Tausig (22), B. visits Wagner (50) at Penzing, spring. Having returned to Hamburg, May, B. receives an invitation to become conductor of the *Singakademie* in Vienna. He settles there in August. Variations on a theme by Schumann for piano duet (Op. 23) published. | Mascagni born, Dec 7 |
| 1864 | 31 | Resigns the conductorship | Meyerbeer (73) dies, May |

| Year | Age | Life | Contemporary Musicians |
|------|-----|------|------------------------|
| | | of the *Singakademie*, but remains permanently in Vienna. Summer holiday spent at Baden-Baden, where Clara Schumann (45) lives. Meeting with Turgeniev (46), who makes a sketch for an opera libretto for him. Sonata, F minor, for two pianos converted into the piano Quintet (Op. 34). | 2; Strauss (R.) born, June 11. |
| 1865 | 32 | Death of B.'s mother (76) in Hamburg, Feb. 2. She had been separated from her husband, whose senior she was by 17 years. Visit to Baden-Baden again, summer, where he composes the horn Trio, E♭ major (Op. 40). Concert tours, including Switzerland, autumn and winter. | Dukas born, Oct. 1; Glazunov born, July 29/Aug. 10; Sibelius born, Dec. 8. |
| 1866 | 33 | German Requiem (Op. 45) worked at Carlsruhe, Feb.-April. After a visit to Switzerland, where the string Quartet in C minor (Op. 51 No. 1) is composed, the Requiem is finished at Baden-Baden, Aug., except No. 5. Tour continued with Joachim (35), Oct., and visit paid at Hamburg to his father (60), who has married again. Return to Vienna, Nov. Variations on a theme of Paganini for piano (Op. | Busoni born, April 1. |

| *Year* | *Age* | *Life* | *Contemporary Musicians* |
|---|---|---|---|
| | | 35), string Sextet, G major (Op. 36), 3 Sacred Choruses for female voices (Op. 37), cello and piano Sonata, E minor (Op. 38), and horn Trio, E♭ major (Op. 40), published. | |
| 1867 | 34 | Two concert tours through the Austrian provinces and to Budapest, spring and autumn, the latter with Joachim (36). First three numbers of the Requiem performed in Vienna, Dec. 1, with little success. Waltzes for piano duet (Op. 39) and 5 Partsongs for male voices (Op. 41) published. | Granados born, July 29. |
| 1868 | 35 | Concert tour with Stockhausen (42), spring. First performance of the complete German Requiem (Op. 45), except No. 5, under Reinthaler (46) at Bremen, April 10. No. 5 added, and the Cantata, *Rinaldo* (Op. 50), composed, summer. The Requiem published, also additional numbers to the *Magelone Romances* (Op. 33), Songs (Opp. 43, 46–9) and Partsongs (Opp. 42 and 44). | Bantock born, Aug. 7; Rossini (76) dies, Nov. 13. |
| 1869 | 36 | First complete performance of the German Requiem, at the Gewandhaus in Leipzig, conducted by Reinecke (45), Feb. 18. *Liebeslieder* | Berlioz (66) dies, March 8; Dargomijsky (56) dies, Jan. 17; Loewe (73) dies, April 20; Pfitzner born, May 5; Roussel born, April 5. |

| Year | Age | Life | Contemporary Musicians |
|------|-----|------|------------------------|
| | | Waltzes for piano duet and vocal quartet (Op. 52) and Rhapsody for contralto, male voice choir and orchestra (Op. 53) composed. Hungarian Dances for piano duet, vols. i and ii, published. | |
| 1870 | 37 | Alto Rhapsody (Op. 53) published, Jan., and first performed, at Jena, March 3. | Balfe (62) dies, Oct. 20; Mercadante (75) dies, Dec. 17; Novák born, Dec. 5; Schmitt (Florent) born, Sept. 28. |
| 1871 | 38 | *Triumphlied* (Op. 55) composed to celebrate the German victory in the Franco-Prussian War, early spring. *Schicksalslied* for chorus and orchestra (Op. 54) finished, May. Songs (Opp. 57 and 58) published. | Auber (89) dies, May 12; Scriabin born, Dec. 25 (O.S.). |
| 1872 | 39 | Death of B.'s father, Johann Jakob Brahms (66) in Hamburg, Feb. 11. First performance of the *Triumphlied* (Op. 55) in its complete form at Carlsruhe under Levi (33). After a holiday at Baden-Baden, B. returns to Vienna, where he is appointed artistic director of the Gesellschaft der Musikfreunde in succession to Rubinstein (42). | Vaughan Williams born, Oct. 12. |
| 1873 | 40 | Variations on a theme of Haydn for orchestra (Op. 56A) or two pianos (Op. | Rachmaninov born, March 20/April 1; Reger born, March 19. |

| Year | Age | *Life* | *Contemporary Musicians* |
|------|-----|--------|--------------------------|
|  |  | 56B). 2 string Quartets (Op. 51) published, autumn. First performance by the Vienna Philharmonic Society of the Haydn Variations in their orchestral version, Nov. 2. Songs (Op. 59) published. |  |
| 1874 | 41 | Visit to Leipzig, where he meets Herzogenberg (31), Spitta (33) and others. Several works performed there. He also goes to Munich and Cologne. Summer holiday spent in Switzerland, near Zürich. Piano Quartet, C minor (Op. 60), finished there and Songs (Op. 63), vocal Quartets (Op. 64) and *Neue Liebeslieder* for piano duet and vocal quartet (Op. 65) taken in hand. 4 vocal Duets (Op. 61) and 7 Partsongs (Op. 62) published, also Opp. 63 and 64. | Cornelius (50) dies, Oct. 26; Holst born, Sept. 21; Schoenberg born, Sept. 13; Suk born, Jan. 4. |
| 1875 | 42 | Resigns the conductorship of the Gesellschaft der Musikfreunde. During a holiday near Heidelberg, B. is occupied with the Symphony No. 1, C minor (Op. 68), and sketches No. 2, D major (Op. 73), summer. Piano Quartet, C minor (Op. 60), published. | Bizet (37) dies, June 3; Ravel born, March 7. |
| 1876 | 43 | String Quartet, B♭ major (Op. 67), finished at Sass- | Falla born, Nov. 23; Götz (36) dies, Dec. 3. |

| Year | Age | Life | Contemporary Musicians |
|------|-----|------|------------------------|
| | | nitz, Isle of Rügen, summer. First performance of Symphony No. 1, C minor (Op. 68), at Carlsruhe, under Dessoff (41), Nov. 4. B. afterwards conducts it at Mannheim and Munich. | |
| 1877 | 44 | Refuses the offer of the honorary doctor's degree made him by the University of Cambridge, not wishing to travel to England to receive it, March. Symphony No. 2, D major (Op. 73), begun at Pörtschach, on the Lake of Wörth, summer, and finished at Lichtenthal near Baden-Baden, autumn . First performance of it by the Vienna Philharmonic Society under Richter (34), Dec. 30. Publication of first Symphony (Op. 68), Songs (Opp. 69–72) and second Symphony (Op. 73). | Dohnányi born, July 27. |
| 1878 | 45 | Visit to Italy, April. During a summer holiday at Pörtschach the piano pieces (Op. 76) and the violin Concerto, D major (Op. 77), are finished. Two Motets for unaccompanied chorus (Op. 74) composed. Second Symphony (Op. 73) and *Balladen und Romanzen* for 2 voices (Op. 75) published. | |
| 1879 | 46 | First performance of the | Bridge (Frank) born, Feb. |

| Year | Age | Life | Contemporary Musicians |
|------|-----|------|------------------------|

violin Concerto, D major (Op. 77), at a Gewandhaus concert in Leipzig, with Joachim (48) as soloist, Jan. 1. Composition of violin and piano Sonata No. 1, G major (Op. 78), and 2 Rhapsodies for piano (Op. 79). The University of Breslau confers the honorary degree of Doctor of Philosophy on B.

26; Ireland born, Aug. 13; Karg-Elert born, Nov. 21; Medtner born, Dec. 4; Respighi born, July 9; Scott (Cyril) born, Sept. 27.

1880  47  *Academic Festival Overture* (Op. 80) and *Tragic Overture* (Op. 81) composed during a summer holiday at Ischl. Publication of the 2 Rhapsodies for piano (Op. 79) and Hungarian Dances for piano duet, vols. iii and iv.

Bloch born, July 24; Offenbach (61) dies, Oct. 4; Pizzetti born, Sept. 20.

1881  48  First performance of the *Academic Festival* and *Tragic Overtures* (Opp. 80 and 81) at Breslau, Jan. 4. Visits to Holland and Hungary, Jan. and Feb. At Budapest B. meets Liszt (70) again after many years. Visit to Sicily, spring. *Nänie* for chorus and orchestra (Op. 82) and piano Concerto No. 2, B♮ major (Op. 83), composed during the summer, at Pressbaum near Vienna. First performance of the Concerto at Stuttgart, with B. as soloist, Nov. 22.

Bartók born, March 25; Miaskovsky born, April 8/20; Mussorgsky (42) dies, March 16/28.

| Year | Age | Life | Contemporary Musicians |
|------|-----|------|------------------------|
| 1882 | 49 | Extensive tour on which he plays the new piano Concerto in many musical centres. Piano Trio, C major (Op. 87), string Quintet, F major (Op. 88) and *Gesang der Parzen* for chorus and orchestra (Op. 89) composed; Symphony No. 3, F major (Op. 90), begun. Songs (Opp. 84–6) published. Visit to Italy, Sept. | Kodály born, Dec. 16; Malipiero born, March 18; Raff (60) dies, June 24–25; Stravinsky born, June 5/17. |
| 1883 | 50 | Symphony No. 3, F major (Op. 90), finished during a summer holiday at Wiesbaden. First performance of the Symphony by the Vienna Philharmonic Society under Richter (40), Dec. 2. | Bax born, Nov. 6; Casella born, July 25; Szymanowski born; Wagner (70) dies, Feb. 13; Webern born, Dec. 3. |
| 1884 | 51 | Composition of the Symphony No. 4, E minor (Op. 98), begun during a holiday at Mürzuschlag in Styria, summer. Publication of third Symphony (Op. 90), 2 Songs for contralto and viola (Op. 91), 4 vocal Quartets (Op. 92), Songs and Romances for chorus (Op. 93) and Songs for voice and piano (Opp. 94 and 95). | Smetana (60) dies, May 12. |
| 1885 | 52 | Symphony No. 4, E minor (Op. 98), finished during another holiday at Mürzuschlag, summer. | Berg born, Feb. 7. |

| Year | Age | Life | Contemporary Musicians |
|------|-----|------|------------------------|
| | | Production of the Symphony at Meiningen, under Bülow (55), Oct. 25. Bülow then takes the work on an important tour with the Meiningen orchestra, including Holland. | |
| 1886 | 53 | Fourth Symphony performed in Vienna, under Richter (43), Jan. 17, and at Leipzig, Feb. 18 and Hamburg, April 9, under B. He goes to Switzerland and lives at Thun, spring–autumn. Cello and piano Sonata, F major (Op. 99), violin and piano Sonata, A major (Op. 100), and piano Trio, C minor (Op. 101), composed there. Songs (Opp. 96 and 97) and fourth Symphony (Op. 98) published. | Liszt (75) dies, July 31. |
| 1887 | 54 | Visit to Italy with Kirchner (64) and the publisher Simrock, spring. He goes to Thun again for the summer. Concerto for violin, cello and orchestra (Op. 102) and Gypsy Songs for vocal quartet and piano (Op. 103) composed there. | Borodin (53) dies, Feb. 16/28. |
| 1888 | 55 | Meeting with Tchaikovsky (48), Jan. Tour in Italy, where Martucci (32) visits him, spring. Third summer spent at Thun, where he | |

| Year | Age | Life | Contemporary Musicians |
|------|-----|------|------------------------|
| | | composes the violin and piano Sonata No. 3, D minor (Op. 108). | |
| 1889 | 56 | The Sonata first performed by Joachim (58) and B. in Vienna, Feb. 13. B. spends the summer at Ischl, near Goldmark (59) and Johann Strauss (64). *Deutsche Fest- und Gedenksprüche* for 8-part chorus (Op. 109) composed for Hamburg in return for the freedom of the city. Leopold Order conferred on B. by the Emperor Francis Joseph (59). 3 Motets (Op. 110) composed. | |
| 1890 | 57 | Visit to Italy, spring. Summer spent at Ischl, where he composes the string Quintet, G major (Op. 111). | Franck (68) dies, Nov. 8; Gade (73) dies, Dec. 21. |
| 1891 | 58 | Having heard Mühlfeld (35) play the clarinet at Meiningen, B. decides to write for the instrument, spring. During a summer holiday at Ischl, he writes the clarinet Trio, A minor (Op. 114), and the clarinet Quintet, B minor (Op. 115). | Bliss born, Aug. 2; Delibes (55) dies, Jan. 16; Prokofiev born, April 11/23. |
| 1892 | 59 | The clarinet works (Opp. 114 and 115) published, also 7 Fantasies (Op. 116) and 3 Intermezzi (Op. 117) for piano. Death of Elisabeth von Herzogenberg (44), Jan. | Franz (77) dies, Oct. 24; Honegger born, March 10; Lalo (69) dies, April 22; Milhaud born, Sept. 4. |
| 1893 | 60 | Visit to Italy, spring. At | Gounod (75) dies, Oct. 18; |

| Year | Age | Life | Contemporary Musicians |
|------|-----|------|------------------------|
| | | Ischl, in the summer, he writes the piano pieces (Opp. 118 and 119) and completes his arrangements of German folksongs. 2 vols. of Technical Exercises for piano published. | Tchaikovsky (53) dies, Oct. 25/Nov. 6. |
| 1894 | 61 | 2 Sonatas for clarinet and piano (Op. 120) composed at Ischl. German folksongs arranged for voice and piano (6 vols.) and solo voice and chorus (1 vol.) published. | Chabrier (53) dies, Sept. 13; Rubinstein (64) dies, Nov. 8/20. |
| 1895 | 62 | Tour in Germany with Mühlfeld (39) to play the clarinet Sonatas, Feb. Summer again spent at Ischl. Visits to a Musical Festival at Meiningen, Sept., to Clara Schumann (76) at Frankfort, Oct. 3, and to Switzerland, Oct. | Hindemith born, Nov. 16. |
| 1896 | 63 | *Vier ernste Gesänge* for voice and piano (Op. 121) composed, May. B. rushes to the funeral of Clara Schumann (77, d. May 20) at Bonn, thus impairing his already precarious health still more, May 24. 11 Preludes for organ (Op. 122) composed, summer. B. is ordered to Carlsbad by his doctor and there his liver is found to be seriously affected, Sept. Returns to Vienna worse than before, Oct. | Bruckner (72) dies, Oct. 11. |

| Year | Age | Life | Contemporary Musicians |
|------|-----|------|------------------------|
| 1897 | 64 | His illness makes alarming progress, Feb. B. appears for the last time at a concert, March 7.<br><br>    Brahms dies in Vienna of cancer, April 3. | Korngold born, May 29. Albeniz aged 37; Balakirev 60; Bantock 29; Bartók 16; Bax 15; Berg 12; Bliss 6; Bloch 17; Boito 55; Bridge (Frank) 18; Bruch 59; Brüll 51; Busoni 31; Casella 14; Chausson 42; Cui 62; Debussy 35; Delius 35; Dohnányi 20; Draeseke 62; Dvořák 56; Dukas 32; Duparc 49; Elgar 40; Falla 21; Fauré 52; Glazunov 32; Goldmark 67; Granados 30; Grieg 54; Hindemith 2; Holst 23; Honegger 5; Humperdinck 43; d'Indy 46; Ireland 18; Karg-Elert 18; Kirchner 74; Kodály 15; Leoncavallo 39; Liadov 42; MacDowell 36; Mackenzie 50; Mahler 37; Malipiero 15; Martucci 41; Mascagni 34; Massenet 55; Medtner 18; Miaskovsky 16; Milhaud 5; Novák 27; Parry 49; Pedrell 56; Pfitzner 28; Pizzetti 17; Prokofiev 6; Puccini 39; Rachmaninov 24; Ravel 22; Reger 24; Respighi 18; Rheinberger 58; Rimsky-Korsakov 53; Roussel 28; Saint-Saëns 62; Schmitt 27; Schönberg, 23; Scott (Cyril) 18; Scriabin 26; Sgambati 54; Sibelius 32; Sinding 41; Smyth |

| *Year* | *Age* | *Life* | *Contemporary Musicians* |
|--------|-------|--------|--------------------------|
|        |       |        | (Ethel) 39; Stainer 57; Stanford 45; Strauss (J. ii) 72; Strauss (R.) 33; Stravinsky 15; Suk 23; Sullivan 55; Svendsen 57; Szymanowski 14; Taneiev 41; Vaughan Williams 25; Verdi 84; Webern 14; Wolf 37. |

# APPENDIX B

THIS catalogue is as complete as I can make it. At one time it was generally believed that Brahms destroyed almost all his unpublished manuscripts before his death. So far as major works are concerned this is probably true; no unknown symphony or full-scale chamber work has come to light since 1897. But those who have consulted the Vienna Philharmonic Society's edition of the Collected Works published in 1926 or 1927 will be aware that its scholarly editors (Eusebius Mandyczewski and Hans Gál) assembled quite a number of minor works—small piano pieces, folksong arrangements and the like—that have been found during the present century. It is at least probable that further gleanings have been made since 1927, and I must apologize that (apart from the 'Ophelia' songs) I do not know what they are.

The dates given for the composition of most of the works are, again, the best I can do. Brahms would begin a major work, lay it aside, take it up again, modify it extensively and eventually send it to the publisher. The whole process might occupy many years. To pretend that during all these years he was continually occupied with the work in question would be ridiculous; but it is often no less ridiculous to single out one or more years and assert that in these the act of composition took place. Small piano pieces and songs Brahms would write when the fancy moved him. The manuscript, when completed, might be put (undated) in his desk to await the moment when a sufficient number of kindred pieces had accumulated to make a set. Then —or perhaps not then, but after some further delay—the whole opus would be released for publication, the order of its numbers being decided on artistic grounds without any regard for chronology. The reader must not be surprised, therefore, to find many dates left blank, others marked with a query, and he is asked to forgive the inevitable vagueness of such an entry as 'from 1858 or earlier.' I wish indeed that I could feel quite sure of my accuracy in all those cases where I have ventured to commit myself to a definite year.

# *Brahms*

## PIANO SOLOS

*Opus.*

1. Sonata in C major (1852–3).
2. Sonata in F♯ minor (1852).
4. Scherzo in E♭ minor (1851).
5. Sonata in F minor (1853).
9. Variations on a Theme by Schumann (1854).
10. Four Ballades (No. 1 in D minor; No. 2 in D major; No. 3 in B minor; No. 4 in B major) (1854).
— Two Gigues (No. 1 in A minor; No. 2 in B minor) (1855).
— Two Sarabandes (No. 1 in A minor; No. 2 in B minor (1855).
21. Variations: No. 1 on an Original Theme (1856); No. 2 on a Hungarian Theme (? 1853).
24. Variations and Fugue on a Theme by Handel (1861).
35. Studies (Variations) on a Theme by Paganini (two sets) (1862–3).
76. Eight Pieces (1878, or earlier):
    Set 1: No. 1, Capriccio (F♯ minor); No. 2, Capriccio (B minor); No. 3, Intermezzo (A♭ major); No. 4, Intermezzo (B♭ major).
    Set 2: No. 5, Capriccio (C♯ minor); No. 6, Intermezzo (A major); No. 7, Intermezzo (A minor); No. 8, Capriccio (C major).
79. Two Rhapsodies (No. 1 in B minor, No. 2 in G minor) (1879).
116. Fantasias (1891–2).
    Set 1: No. 1. Capriccio (D minor); No. 2, Intermezzo (A minor); No. 3, Capriccio (G minor).
    Set 2: No. 4, Intermezzo (E major); No. 5, Intermezzo (E minor); No. 6, Intermezzo (E major); No. 7, Capriccio (D minor).
117. Three Intermezzi (No. 1 in E♭ major, No. 2 in B♭ minor, No. 3 in C♯ minor) (1892).
118. Six Pieces (1893).
    No. 1, Intermezzo (A minor); No. 2, Intermezzo (A major); No. 3, Ballade (G minor); No. 4, Intermezzo (F minor); No. 5, Romanze (F major); No. 6, Intermezzo (E♭ minor)

# Appendix B—Catalogue of Works

Brahms never claimed to have invented the melodies of the Hungarian Dances, though some of them may be his own.

# Brahms

## Arrangements for Piano Duet

Opus.

52A. *Liebeslieder* Waltzes (see Vocal Quartets) (1868 or 1869).

65A. *Neue Liebeslieder* (see Vocal Quartets) (1874).

### TWO PIANOS

34B. Sonata in F minor (an earlier version of the piano Quintet, Op. 34) (?).

56B. Variations on a Theme by Haydn (for the alternative (orchestral) version see Orchestral Works) (1873).

### ORGAN WORKS

— Two Preludes and Fugues:
      No. 1, in A minor (1856).
      No. 2, in G minor (1857).
— Fugue in A♭ minor (c. 1857).
— Chorale Prelude and Fugue, *O Traurigkeit* (A minor) (c. 1857).

122. Eleven Chorale Preludes (1896, but some may be earlier).

> No. 1, Mein Jesu, der du mich; No. 2, Herzliebster Jesu; No. 3, O Welt, ich muss dich lassen; No. 4, Herzlich tut mich erfreuen; No. 5, Schmücke dich, O liebe Seele; No. 6, O wie selig seid ihr doch; No. 7, O Gott, du frommer Gott; No. 8, Es ist ein Ros' entsprungen; Nos. 9 and 10, Herzlich tut mich verlangen; No. 11, O Welt, ich muss dich lassen.

### CHAMBER MUSIC

— Sonatensatz. Scherzo in C minor for violin and pianoforte, from a Sonata written jointly with Schumann and Dietrich (1853).

8. Trio in B major for violin, cello and pianoforte (1853–4).
    The same, revised (1891).

18. Sextet in B♭ major for 2 violins, 2 violas and 2 cellos (1859–60).

25. Quartet in G minor for violin, viola, cello and pianoforte (completed 1861).

26. Quartet in A major for violin, viola, cello and pianoforte (1861–2).

34. Quintet in F minor for 2 violins, viola, cello and pianoforte (1864).

36. Sextet in G major for 2 violins, 2 violas and 2 cellos (1864–5).

38. Sonata in E minor for cello and pianoforte (1862–5).

40. Trio in E♭ major for violin, horn (or cello or viola) and pianoforte (1865).

# Appendix B—Catalogue of Works

**Opus.**

51. Two Quartets for 2 violins, viola and cello: No. 1 in C minor; No. 2 in A minor (completed 1873).
60. Quartet in C minor for violin, viola, cello and pianoforte (completed 1874 or 1875).
67. Quartet in B♭ major for 2 violins, viola and cello (? 1875).
78. Sonata in G major for violin and pianoforte (1879).
87. Trio in C major for violin, cello and pianoforte (1882).
88. Quintet in F major for 2 violins, 2 violas and cello (1882).
99. Sonata in F major for cello and pianoforte (1886).
100. Sonata in A major for violin and pianoforte (1886).
101. Trio in C minor for violin, cello and pianoforte (1886).
108. Sonata in D minor for violin and pianoforte (1886–8).
111. Quintet in G major for 2 violins, 2 violas and cello (? 1890).
114. Trio in A minor for clarinet (or viola), cello and pianoforte (1891).
115. Quintet in B minor for clarinet, 2 violins, viola and cello (1891).
120. Two Sonatas for clarinet (or viola or violin) and pianoforte: No. 1 in F minor, No. 2 in E♭ major (1894).

## ORCHESTRAL WORKS

11. Serenade in D major (1857 or 1858).
15. First pianoforte Concerto, in D minor (1854–8).
16. Serenade in A major for small orchestra (without violins) (completed 1859, revised 1875).
56A. Variations on a Theme by Haydn, in B♭ major (1873).
68. First Symphony, in C minor (completed 1876).
73. Second Symphony, in D major (completed 1877).
77. Violin Concerto in D major (1878).
80. Academic Festival Overture (1880).
81. Tragic Overture (completed 1880).
83. Second pianoforte Concerto, in B♭ major (completed 1881).
90. Third Symphony, in F major (completed 1883).
98. Fourth Symphony, in E minor (completed 1885).
102. Double Concerto in A minor for violin and cello (1887).

### Arrangement for Orchestra

Hungarian Dances, Nos. 1, 3 and 10 (from the sets for pianoforte duet).

# Brahms

*Opus.*

3. 6 Songs (1853 or earlier):
   1. Liebestreu — Robert Reinick
   2. Liebe und Frühling, I ⎫ Hoffmann von
   3. Liebe und Frühling, II ⎭ Fallersleben
   4. Lied aus dem Gedicht 'Ivan' — Bodenstedt
   5. In der Fremde — Eichendorff
   6. Lied — Eichendorff

6. 6 Songs (1853 or earlier):
   1. Spanisches Lied — Paul Heyse
   2. Der Frühling — J. B. Rousseau
   3. Nachwirkung — Alfred Meissner
   4. Juchhe! — Reinick
   5. Wie die Wolke nach der Sonne — Hoffmann von Fallersleben
   6. Nachtigallen schwingen — Hoffmann von Fallersleben

7. 6 Songs (1853 or earlier):
   1. Treue Liebe — Ferrand
   2. Parole — Eichendorff
   3. Anklänge — Eichendorff
   4. Volkslied — Traditional
   5. Die Trauernde — Traditional
   6. Heimkehr — Uhland

— 'Mondnacht' (? 1854) — Eichendorff

14. 8 Songs and Romances (c. 1858):
    1. Vor dem Fenster — Traditional
    2. Vom verwundeten Knaben — Traditional
    3. Murrays Ermordung — Herder, from the Scottish
    4. Ein Sonett — 13th Century
    5. Trennung — Traditional
    6. Gang zur Liebsten — Traditional
    7. Ständchen — Traditional
    8. Sehnsucht — Traditional

19. 5 Poems (1858-9)
    1. Der Kuss — Hölty
    2. Scheiden und Meiden — Uhland
    3. In der Ferne — Uhland

**Opus.**

4. Der Schmied             Uhland
5. An eine Aeolsharfe      Eduard Mörike

32. 9 Songs: (? 1864):

### SET I

1. Wie rafft' ich mich auf in der    August von Platen
   Nacht
2. Nicht mehr zu dir zu gehen    G. F. Daumer
3. Ich schleich' umher betrübt    Platen
   und stumm
4. Der Strom, der neben mir    Platen
   verrauschte

### SET II

5. Wehe, so willst du mich    Platen
   wieder
6. Du sprichst, dass ich mich    Platen
   täuschte
7. Bitteres zu sagen          Daumer, after Hafiz
8. So stehn wir              Daumer, after Hafiz
9. Wie bist du, meine Königin   Daumer, after Hafiz

33. 15 Romances from 'Magelone'   Ludwig Tieck
    (1861–8)

### SET I

1. Keinen hat es noch gereut
2. Traun! Bogen und Pfeil
3. Sind es Schmerzen

### SET II

4. Liebe kam aus fernen Landen
5. So willst du des Armen
6. Wie soll ich die Freude

### SET III

7. War es dir
8. Wir müssen uns trennen
9. Ruhe, Süssliebchen

*Opus.*

6. Vergangen ist mir Glück und   Old German
Heil

7. Herbstgefühl               A. F. von Schack

49. 5 Songs (1868 and earlier):

1. Am Sonntag Morgen     Heyse, from 'Italienisches
Liederbuch'

2. An ein Veilchen          Hölty

3. Sehnsucht               From the Czech

4. Wiegenlied (to B. F. in   G. Scherer
Vienna)

5. Abenddämmerung        Schack

57. 8 Songs (1871):           G. F. Daumer

### SET I

1. Von waldbekränzter Höhe
2. Wenn du nur zuweilen lächelst
3. Es träumte mir
4. Ach, wende diesen Blick

### SET II

5. In meiner Nächte Sehnen
6. Strahlt zuweilen
7. Die Schnur, die Perl' an Perle
8. Unbewegte laue Luft

58. 8 Songs (1871):

### SET I

1. Blinde Kuh            August Kopisch, from the
Italian

2. Während des Regens    Kopisch

3. Die Spröde            Kopisch, from the Calabrian

4. O komme, holde Sommer-   M. Grohe
nacht

### SET II

5. Schwermut           Carl Candidus
6. In der Gasse         Friedrich Hebbel
7. Vorüber              Hebbel
8. Serenade            Schack

# Brahms

59. 8 Songs (1871–3):

SET I

|   |   |   |
|---|---|---|
| 1. | Dämm'rung senkte sich von oben | Goethe |
| 2. | Auf dem See | Carl Simrock |
| 3. | Regenlied | Klaus Groth |
| 4. | Nachklang | Groth |

SET II

|   |   |   |
|---|---|---|
| 5. | Agnes | Mörike |
| 6. | Eine gute, gute Nacht | Daumer |
| 7. | Mein wundes Herz | Groth |
| 8. | Dein blaues Auge | Groth |

— 5 Songs of Ophelia from 'Hamlet' (1873).     Shakespeare

63. 9 Songs (1873–4):

SET I

|   |   |   |
|---|---|---|
| 1. | Frühlingstrost | Max von Schenkendorf |
| 2. | Erinnerung | Schenkendorf |
| 3. | An ein Bild | Schenkendorf |
| 4. | An die Tauben | Schenkendorf |

SET II

|   |   |   |
|---|---|---|
| 5. | Junge Lieder, I ('Meine Liebe ist grün') | Felix Schumann |
| 6. | Junge Lieder, II ('Wenn um den Hollunder') | Felix Schumann |
| 7. | Heimweh, I ('Wie traulich war') | Groth |
| 8. | Heimweh, II ('O wüsst ich doch') | Groth |
| 9. | Heimweh, III ('Ich sah als Knabe') | Groth |

69. 9 Songs (1877):

SET I

|   |   |   |
|---|---|---|
| 1. | Klage, I | Joseph Wenzig, from the Czech |
| 2. | Klage, II | Wenzig, from the Slovak |

*Opus.*

| | | |
|---|---|---|
| 3. | Abschied | Wenzig, from the Czech |
| 4. | Des Liebsten Schwur | Wenzig, from the Czech |
| 5. | Tambourliedchen | Carl Candidus |

SET II

| | | |
|---|---|---|
| 6. | Vom Strande | Eichendorff, from the Spanish |
| 7. | Über die See | Carl Lemcke |
| 8. | Salome | Gottfried Keller |
| 9. | Mädchenfluch | Kapper, from the Serbian |

70. 4 Songs (1875–7):

| | | |
|---|---|---|
| 1. | Im Garten am Seegestade | Lemcke |
| 2. | Lerchengesang | Candidus |
| 3. | Serenate | Goethe |
| 4. | Abendregen | Keller |

71. 5 Songs (1877):

| | | |
|---|---|---|
| 1. | Es liebt sich so lieblich | Heine |
| 2. | An den Mond | Simrock |
| 3. | Geheimnis | Candidus |
| 4. | Willst du, dass ich geh' | Lemcke |
| 5. | Minnelied | Hölty |

72. 5 Songs (1876–7):

| | | |
|---|---|---|
| 1. | Alte Liebe | Candidus |
| 2. | Sommerfäden | Candidus |
| 3. | O kühler Wald | C. Brentano |
| 4. | Verzagen | Lemcke |
| 5. | Unüberwindlich | Goethe |

84. 5 Songs and Romances (*see also* Vocal Duets) (? 1878–81):

| | | |
|---|---|---|
| 1. | Sommerabend | Hans Schmidt |
| 2. | Der Kranz | Schmidt |
| 3. | In den Beeren | Schmidt |
| 4. | Vergebliches Ständchen (Lower Rhenish) | Traditional |
| 5. | Spannung (Lower Rhenish) | Traditional |

85. 6 Songs (? 1877–9):

| | | |
|---|---|---|
| 1. | Sommerabend | Heine |
| 2. | Mondenschein | Heine |

*Opus.*

    3. Mädchenlied                Siegfried Kapper, from the Serbian

    4. Ade!                       Kapper, from the Czech

    5. Frühlingslied             Geibel

    6. In Waldeseinsamkeit     Lemcke

86. 6 Songs (1877–8):

    1. Therese                 Keller

    2. Feldeinsamkeit        Hermann Allmers

    3. Nachtwandler         Max Kalbeck

    4. Über die Haide       Theodor Storm

    5. Versunken           Felix Schumann

    6. Todessehnen         Schenkendorf

91. 2 Songs for contralto with viola *obbligato* (1884 or earlier):

    1. Gestillte Sehnsucht    Rückert

    2. Geistliches Wiegenlied  Geibel, after Lope de Vega

94. 5 Songs (1884):

    1. Mit vierzig Jahren     Rückert

    2. Steig auf, geliebter Schatten  Friedrich Halm

    3. Mein Herz ist schwer   Geibel

    4. Sapphische Ode       Schmidt

    5. Kein Haus, keine Heimat  Halm, from a drama

95. 7 Songs (1884):

    1. Das Mädchen        Kapper, from the Serbian

    2. Bei dir sind meine Gedanken  Halm

    3. Beim Abschied (2 versions)  Halm

    4. Der Jäger            Halm

    5. Vorschneller Schwur    Kapper, from the Serbian

    6. Mädchenlied          Heyse, from the Italian

    7. Schön war, das ich dir weihte  Daumer

96. 4 Songs (? 1884–6):

    1. Der Tod, das ist die kühle Nacht  Heine

    2. Wir wandelten        Daumer

    3. Es schauen die Blumen   Heine

    4. Meerfahrt           Heine

*Opus.*

97. 6 Songs (1884–6):
    1. Nachtigall — C. Reinhold
    2. Auf dem Schiffe — Reinhold
    3. Entführung — Willibald Alexis
    4. Dort in den Weiden (Lower Rhenish) — Traditional
    5. Komm bald — Groth
    6. Trennung (Swabian) — Traditional

105. 5. Songs (? 1886):
    1. Wie Melodien zieht es — Groth
    2. Immer leiser wird mein Schlummer — Hermann Lingg
    3. Klage (Lower Rhenish) — Traditional
    4. Auf dem Kirchhofe — Detlev von Liliencron
    5. Verrat — Lemcke

106. 5 Songs (? 1886–9):
    1. Ständchen — Franz Kugler
    2. Auf dem See — Reinhold
    3. Es hing der Reif — Groth
    4. Meine Lieder — Adolf Frey
    5. Ein Wanderer — Reinhold

107. 5 Songs (? 1886–9):
    1. An die Stolze — Flemming
    2. Salamander — Lemcke
    3. Das Mädchen spricht — O. F. Gruppe
    4. Maienkätzchen — Liliencron
    5. Mädchenlied — Heyse

121. 'Vier ernste Gesänge' (1896): — Biblical
    1. Denn es gehet dem Menschen
    2. Ich wandte mich und sahe
    3. O Tod, wie bitter
    4. Wenn ich mit Menschen und mit Engelzungen

— 'Regenlied' (?) — Groth

*Arrangement for Voice and Piano*

103. Eight Gypsy Songs (from the Vocal Quartets) (?)

# Brahms

### *Arrangements for Voice and Orchestra*

— Memnon (Schubert, Op. 6) (1862)
— An Schwager Kronos (Schubert) (1862)
— Geheimes (Schubert, Op. 14 No. 2)

## VOCAL DUETS

20. 3 Duets for soprano and contralto (*c.* 1858–60):
    1. Weg der Liebe, I   &#125;    Herder, from 'Stimmen der
    2. Weg der Liebe, II  &#125;      Völker'
    3. Die Meere              'From the Italian'

28. 4 Duets for contralto and baritone (1860–2)
    1. Die Nonne und der Ritter    Eichendorff
    2. Vor der Tür               Old German
    3. Es rauschet das Wasser      Goethe
    4. Der Jäger und sein Liebchen   Hoffmann von Fallersleben

61. 4 Duets for soprano and contralto (1874): ·
    1. Die Schwestern       Mörike
    2. Klosterfräulein        Justinus Kerner
    3. Phänomen            Goethe
    4. Die Boten der Liebe     Wenzig, from the Czech

66. 5 Duets for soprano and contralto (?):
    1. Klänge, I               Groth
    2. Klänge, II             Groth
    3. Am Strande            Hölty
    4. Jägerlied               Candidus
    5. Hüt' du dich           From 'Des Knaben Wun-
                                     derhorn'

75. 4 Ballads and Romances (1877–8):
    1. Edward (contralto and tenor)   From Herder's 'Volks-
                                     lieder'
    2. Guter Rat (soprano and   From 'Des Knaben Wun-
       contralto)                   derhorn'
    3. So lass uns wandern (soprano   Wenzig, from the Czech
       and contralto)
    4. Walpurgisnacht (2 sopranos)   Willibald Alexis

84. 5 Songs and Romances, for 1 or 2 voices (*see* Songs)

## *Appendix B—Catalogue of Works*

### VOCAL QUARTETS [1]

*Opus.*

31. 3 Quartets, with pianoforte (between 1859–63):
    1. Wechsellied zum Tanze     Goethe
    2. Neckereien (Moravian)     Traditional
    3. Der Gang zum Liebchen   Traditional
       (Czech)

52. 'Liebeslieder,' waltzes for pianoforte   Daumer
    duet with voices *ad lib.* (? 1868–9)

64. 3 Quartets, with pianoforte (between 1862–74):
    1. An die Heimat     C. O. Sternau
    2. Der Abend     Schiller
    3. Fragen     Daumer

65. 'Neue Liebslieder,' waltzes with   Daumer (final
    pianoforte duet (1874 or earlier)    number Goethe)

92. 4 Quartets with pianoforte (1874–84):
    1. O schöne Nacht     Daumer
    2. Spätherbst     Allmers
    3. Abendlied     Hebbel
    4. Warum?     Goethe

103. 'Zigeunerlieder' (Gypsy Songs),    From the Hungarian of
     with pianoforte (1887):     H. Conrat
     1. He, Zigeuner
     2. Hochgetürmte Rimaflut
     3. Wisst ihr, wann mein Kind-
        chen
     4. Lieber Gott, du weisst
     5. Brauner Bursche
     6. Röslein dreie
     7. Kommt dir manchmal in
        den Sinn
     8. Horch, der Wind klagt
     9. Weit und breit
     10. Mond verhüllt sein Angesicht
     11. Rote Abendwolken ziehn

---

[1] All for soprano, contralto, tenor and bass.

# Brahms

*Opus.*

112. 6 Quartets with pianoforte (1888–91):
   1. Sehnsucht                 F. Kugler
   2. Nächtens                 Kugler
   3. Himmel strahlt so helle ⎫
   4. Rote Rosenknospen     ⎬ 'Zigeunerlieder'  (H.
   5. Brennessel steht am Wegesrand ⎪    Conrat)
   6. Liebe Schwalbe ⎭

### CHORAL WORKS (ACCOMPANIED)

12. 'Ave Maria' for female voices, Liturgical
   orchestra or organ (1858)

13. 'Funeral Hymn' for mixed voices (?)
   and wind band (? 1858)

17. Partsongs for female voices, 2 horns and harp (1860):
   1. Es tönt ein voller Harfenklang   Ruperti
   2. Song from 'Twelfth Night'       Shakespeare
   3. Der Gärtner                  Eichendorff
   4. Gesang aus Fingal         Ossian

27. Psalm XIII for female voices and    Biblical
   organ (or pianoforte) (? 1859)

30. Sacred Song 'Lass dich nur nichts    Paul Flemming
   dauern' for mixed voices and
   organ (or pianoforte) (Between
   1856 and 1860)

44. (With pianoforte *ad lib.*, *see* Choral
   Works (Unaccompanied) )

45. 'Ein deutsches Requiem' for soprano   From Luther's translation
   and baritone solo, chorus and       of the Bible
   orchestra (1857–68)

50. Cantata 'Rinaldo' for tenor, male    Goethe
   chorus and orchestra (1863–8)

53. 'Rhapsodie' (fragment from 'Harz-   Goethe
   reise im Winter') for contralto
   solo, male chorus and orchestra
   (1869)

54. 'Schicksalslied' for chorus and orchestra (1868–71) — Hölderlin

55. 'Triumphlied' for chorus and orchestra (1870–1) — Revelation of St. John

— 'Kleine Hochzeitskantate' for 4-part chorus and pianoforte (1874) — Gottfried Keller

82. 'Nänie' for chorus and orchestra (1880–1) — Schiller

89. 'Gesang der Parzen' (from 'Iphigenie auf Tauris') for chorus and orchestra (1882) — Goethe

93B. 'Tafellied (Dank der Damen'), drinking-glee for 6-part chorus and pianoforte (1884) — Eichendorff

### CHORAL WORKS (UNACCOMPANIED)

22. 'Marienlieder' for 4-part mixed voices (? 1859) — ? Traditional
    1. Der englische Gruss
    2. Marias Kirchgang
    3. Marias Wallfahrt
    4. Der Jäger
    5. Ruf zur Maria
    6. Magdalena
    7. Marias Lob

29. 2 Motets for 5-part mixed voices (probably 1860 or earlier):
    1. Chorale 'Es ist das Heil' and Fugue — Paul Speratus (1484–1551)
    2. Schaffe in mir, Gott — Psalm LI

37. 3 Sacred Choruses for female voices: — Liturgical
    1. O bone Jesu
    2. Adoramus te
    3. Regina coeli

41. 5 Partsongs for male voices (1861–2):
    1. Ich schwing mein Horn ins Jammertal — Old German
    2. Freiwillige her! — Carl Lemcke
    3. Geleit — Lemcke

*Opus.*

    4. Marschieren                Lemcke
    5. Gebt Acht!                Lemcke

42. 3 Partsongs for 6-part mixed voices (? 1859–61):
    1. Abendständchen        Clemens Brentano
    2. Vineta                  Wilhelm Müller
    3. Darthulas Grabesgesang  Ossian, translator Herder

44. 12 Songs and Romances for female voices (with pianoforte *ad lib.*) (1866 and earlier):

PART I

    1. Minnelied             J. H. Voss
    2. Der Bräutigam       Eichendorff
    3. Barcarole             Traditional Italian
    4. Fragen               Traditional Slav
    5. Die Müllerin         Adalbert von Chamisso
    6. Die Nonne           Uhland

PART II

    1. Nun stehn die Rosen
    2. Die Berge sind spitz
    3. Am Wildbach die Weiden   } From Paul Heyse's 'Jung-
    4. Und gehst du über den      brunnen'
       Kirchhof
    5. Die Braut             Müller
    6. Märznacht           Uhland

62. 7 Partsongs for mixed voices (1874):
    1. Rosmarin            } From 'Des Knaben Wun-
    2. Von alten Liebesliedern    derhorn'
    3. Waldesnacht
    4. Dein Herzlein mild      } From Heyse's 'Jung-
    5. All' meine Herzgedanken   brunnen'
    6. Es geht ein Wehen
    7. Vergangen ist mir Glück und  Old German
      Heil

74. 2 Motets for mixed chorus (1860–75):
    1. Warum ist das Licht gegeben?  Luther
    2. O Heiland, reiss die Himmel  Anon.
      auf

*Opus.*

93A. 6 Songs and Romances for mixed chorus (? 1883–4):

| | |
|---|---|
| 1. Der bucklichte Fiedler | Rhenish Folksong |
| 2. Das Mädchen | Siegfried Kapper (Serbian) |
| 3. O süsser Mai | L. Achim von Arnim |
| 4. Fahr wohl | Rückert |
| 5. Der Falke | Kapper (Serbian) |
| 6. Beherzigung | Goethe |

104. 5 Partsongs for mixed chorus (1888):

| | |
|---|---|
| 1. Nachtwache: 'Leise Töne der Brust' | Rückert |
| 2. Nachtwache: 'Ruhn sie?' | Rückert |
| 3. Letztes Glück | Max Kalbeck |
| 4. Verlorene Jugend | J. Wenzig, from the Czech |
| 5. Im Herbst | Klaus Groth |

109. 'Fest￢ und Gedenksprüche' Biblical (? 1886–8):

1. Unsere Väter hofften auf dich
2. Wenn ein starker Gewappneter
3. Wo ist ein so herrlich Volk

110. 3 Motets for 4￢ and 8￢part mixed chorus (1889):

| | |
|---|---|
| 1. Ich aber bin elend | Biblical |
| 2. Ach, arme Welt | Anon. |
| 3. Wenn wir in höchsten Nöten sind | Paul Eber (1550) |

— Dem Dunkeln Schoss der Heil'gen Erde (for four￢part chorus) (?) Schiller ('Lied von der Glocke')

## Choral Arrangements

— Gruppe aus dem Tartarus (Schubert, Op. 24 No. 1) (Schiller) for unison male￢voice choir and orchestra
— Ellens zweiten Gesang (Schubert, Op. 52 No. 2) (Storck) (from Sir W. Scott)) for soprano solo, female chorus, 4 horns and 2 bassoons

# Brahms

## CANONS

NOTE. Some of the Op. 113 canons were written before 1862 and may be products of the contrapuntal studies that Brahms and Joachim pursued together. No canon in this set is a late work. *Spruch* was written at Detmold. Concerning the date of the remaining canons I have no information.

## FOLKSONG ARRANGEMENTS FOR 4-PART CHORUS UNACCOMPANIED

14 Deutsche Volkslieder (? 1864):

### BOOK I

# Appendix B—Catalogue of Works

8. In stiller Nacht
9. Abschiedslied
10. Der tote Knabe
11. Die Wollust in den Mayen
12. Morgengesang
13. Schnitter Tod
14. Der englische Jäger

### ADDITIONAL NUMBERS (? 1864)

15. Scheiden
16. Wach auf!
17. Erlaube mir
18. Der Fiedler
19. Da unten im Tale
20. Des Abends
21. Wach auf!
22. Dort in den Weiden
23. Altes Volkslied ('Verstohlen geht der Mond auf')
24. Der Ritter und die Feine
25. Der Zimmergesell
26. Altdeutsches Kampflied ('Wir stehen hier zur Schlacht bereit').
    *See also* '49 Deutsche Volkslieder,' Book VII, *below*

## FOLKSONG ARRANGEMENTS FOR SOLO VOICE AND PIANOFORTE

Volks-Kinderlieder (1858 or earlier):

1. Dornröschen
2. Die Nachtigall
3. Die Henne
4. Sandmännchen
5. Der Mann
6. Heidenröslein
7. Das Schlaraffenland
8A. Beim Ritt auf dem Knie ('Ull Mann wull riden')
8B. Beim Ritt auf dem Knie ('Alt Mann wollt reiten')
9. Der Jäger im Walde
10. Das Mädchen und die Hasel

11. Wiegenlied
12. Weihnachten
13. Marienwürmchen
14. Dem Schutzengel

28 Deutsche Volkslieder (1858):

1. Die Schnürbrust
2. Der Jäger
3. Drei Vögelein
4. Auf, gebet uns das Pfingstei
5. Des Markgrafen Töchterlein
6. Der Reiter
7. Die heilige Elisabeth an ihrem Hochzeitsfeste
8. Der englische Gruss
9. Ich stund an einem Morgen
10. Gunhilde
11. Der tote Gast
12. Tageweis von einer schönen Frauen
13. Schifferlied
14. Nachtgesang
15. Die beiden Königskinder
16. Scheiden
17. Altes Minnelied
18A. Der getreue Eckart
18B. Der getreue Eckart
19. Die Versuchung
20. Der Tochter Wunsch
21. Schnitter Tod
22. Marias Wallfahrt
23. Das Mädchen und der Tod
24. Es ritt ein Ritter wohl durch das Ried
25. Liebeslied
26. Guten Abend, mein tausiger Schatz
27. Der Wollust in den Maien
28. Es reit' ein Herr und auch sein Knech:

49 Deutsche Volkslieder (various dates):

31. Dort in den Weiden steht ein Haus
32. So will ich frisch und fröhlich sein
33. Och Moder, ich well en Ding han!
34. Wie komm ich denn zur Tür herein?
35. Soll sich der Mond nicht heller scheinen

### BOOK VI

36. Es wohnt ein Fiedler
37. Du mein einzig Licht
38. Des Abends kann ich nicht schlafen gehn
39. Schöner Augen, schöne Strahlen
40. Ich weiss mir'n Maidlein hübsch und fein
41. Es steht ein Lind
42. In stiller Nacht, zur ersten Wacht

### BOOK VII (with 4-part chorus *ad lib.*)

43. Es stunden drei Rosen
44. Dem Himmel will ich klagen
45. Es sass ein schneeweiss Vögelein
46. Es war einmal ein Zimmergesell
47. Es ging sich unsre Fraue
48. Nachtigall, sag, was für Grüss
49. Verstohlen geht der Mond auf

Besides writing these original works and arrangements Brahms edited the clavier works of Couperin for Chrysander's *Denkmäler der Tonkunst*, revised Mozart's Requiem for the new edition of Mozart's works, was concerned in the complete edition of Chopin's works, and edited three posthumous works by Schubert and the *Scherzo* and *Presto Appassionato* by Schumann. He also edited some of Bach's works, amplified the figured bass of two Sonatas for violin and clavier by C. P. E. Bach, and furnished the accompaniments to an edition of Handel's vocal duets.

# APPENDIX C

*Albert, Eugène d'* (1864–1932), German pianist and composer of Scottish birth and French descent. He was educated musically in London and Vienna, and finished his piano studies under Liszt. His best-known work is the opera *Tiefland*.

*Barbi, Alice* (1862–?), Italian mezzo-soprano singer and violinist. She made her first appearance at Milan in 1882 and later sang in German as well as in Italian.

*Brendel, Karl Franz* (1811–68), German critic at Leipzig, editor of the *Neue Zeitschrift für Musik* from 1845.

*Bruch, Max* (1838–1920), German composer, professor of composition in Berlin in 1892–1910.

*Brüll, Ignaz* (1846–1907), Austrian pianist and composer in Vienna, author of several operas, the most successful of which was *Das goldene Kreuz* (1875).

*Bülow, Hans von* (1830–94), German pianist and conductor, first husband of Cosima Wagner. Wholly devoted to the cause of Wagner and the 'New German School' at first, later leaning towards Brahms.

*Chrysander, Friedrich* (1826–1901), German musical scholar and editor. He began a large work on Handel, which he did not live to finish, and was intimately concerned with the complete German edition of Handel's works.

*Cossel, Otto Friedrich Willibald,* German pianist at Hamburg, Brahms's first teacher.

*Daumer, Georg Friedrich* (1800–75), German minor poet and philosopher.

*Dietrich, Albert Hermann* (1829–1908), German composer and conductor, court musical director at Oldenburg from 1861.

*Door, Anton* (1833–1919), Austrian pianist, pupil of Czerny and Sechter. He taught in Moscow for a time, but returned to Vienna, where he became piano professor at the Conservatoire.

*Dustmann, Luise* (born *Meyer*) (1831–99), German soprano singer. She was attached to the Vienna Court Opera and as teacher of singing to the Conservatoire.

# Brahms

*Eichendorff, Joseph von* (1788–1857), German romantic poet and novelist, whose poems were set by Schumann, Brahms, and particularly Hugo Wolf.

*Epstein, Julius* (1832–1918), Austrian (Croatian) pianist, professor at the Vienna Conservatoire from 1867 to 1901.

*Feuerbach, Anselm* (1829–80), German painter, mainly of classical subjects.

*Franz, Robert* (1815–92), German composer who lived at Halle, one of the chief representatives of the German *Lied,* ranking immediately below Schubert, Schumann, Brahms and Wolf in that line.

*Friedländer, Max* (1852–1934), German baritone singer and writer on music. He studied with Garcia and Stockhausen (*q.v.*) and taught at the universities of Berlin and Harvard.

*Gänsbacher, Joseph* (1829–1911), Austrian singing-master and cellist. He taught singing at the Vienna Conservatoire.

*Goldmark, Karl* (1830–1915), Hungarian composer settled in Vienna, among whose works the opera *Die Königin von Saba* (*The Queen of Sheba*) and the symphony *Ländliche Hochzeit* (*Rustic Wedding*) are best known.

*Grädener, Karl Georg Peter* (1812–83), German cellist, conductor and composer. After conducting appointments at Kiel and Hamburg, he held one as professor at the Vienna Conservatoire in 1862–5, and a similar one at that of Hamburg from 1867.

*Grimm, Otto Julius* (1827–1903), German pianist and composer, successively at Göttingen and Münster in Westphalia.

*Groth, Klaus* (1819–99), German poet who wrote much of his work in Low German. Professor of literature at Kiel.

*Hanslick, Eduard* (1825–1904), Austrian music critic in Vienna and lecturer on musical history at the University. He was hostile to Wagner and somewhat indiscriminately enthusiastic about Brahms.

*Hausmann, Robert* (1852–1909), German cellist, member of the Joachim Quartet from 1879.

*Hellmesberger, Joseph* (1828–93), Austrian violinist, professor of his instrument at the Vienna Conservatoire and its director from 1851. Conductor of the Gesellschaft der Musikfreunde until 1859 and leader of the Court Opera orchestra from 1860.

*Henschel, Georg* (afterwards *Sir George*) (1850–1934), German singer, composer and conductor long settled in Great Britain and naturalized.

*Herbeck, Johann* (1831–77), Austrian conductor. He succeeded Hellmesberger (*q.v.*) as conductor of the Gesellschaft der Musikfreunde in Vienna and became director of the Court Opera in 1871.

*Herz, Henri* (1802 or 1806–88), Austrian pianist long settled in Paris; composer of shallow virtuoso music for his instrument.

*Herzogenberg, Elisabeth von* (born *von Stockhausen*) (1848–92), German amateur pianist, pupil and friend of Brahms, wife of Heinrich von Herzogenberg (*q.v.*).

*Herzogenberg, Heinrich von* (1843–1900), Austrian composer and conductor long settled at Leipzig.

*Heuberger, Richard* (1850–1914), Austrian critic and composer, mainly of light operas, of which *Der Opernball* was the most famous.

*Hölderlin, Johann Christian Friedrich* (1770–1843), German poet who combined a romantic outlook with a classical manner.

*Joachim, Amalie* (born *Schneeweiss*, called *Weiss*) (1839–98), German contralto singer, married to Joachim (*q.v.*) in 1863.

*Joachim, Joseph* (1831–1907), Hungarian violinist and composer living successively at Leipzig, Weimar, Hanover and Berlin, a frequent visitor to England, founder of the Joachim Quartet in 1869 and head of one of the musical departments of the Royal Academy of Arts in Berlin.

*Kalbeck, Max* (1850–1921), Austrian music critic, author and translator of opera librettos (including Bizet's *Carmen*); author of the first full Brahms biography.

*Labor, Josef* (1842–1924), Austrian (Bohemian) pianist and organist. He studied at the Vienna Conservatoire and, although blind, became chamber musician to the King of Hanover, but lived in Vienna from 1868.

*Levi, Hermann* (1839–1900), German conductor. He studied at Munich and Leipzig, and after various appointments was musical director of the Munich Court Opera in 1872–96. Although a Jew, he was chosen by Wagner to conduct the first performance of *Parsifal* at Bayreuth.

*Loewe, Karl* (1796–1869), German composer. Regarded by many German authorities as one of the chief early exponents of the German *Lied*, he actually cultivated what has always remained one of its mere side-lines—a narrative and picturesque ballad of a peculiarly naïve type which never found acceptance in other countries.

*Mandyczewski, Eusebius* (1857–1929), Austrian musicologist. He became keeper of the archives of the Gesellschaft der Musikfreunde in

Vienna in 1800 and professor at the Conservatoire there in 1897. Editor of the complete editions of Schubert, Brahms and Haydn (the last left unfinished to this day).

*Marxsen, Eduard* (1806–87), German pianist and composer at Hamburg, Brahms's second teacher.

*May, Florence* (1845–1915), English pianist, daughter of the organist and singing-teacher Edward Collett May. She went to Vienna to become a pupil of Brahms, many of whose works she afterwards played in England, and she wrote a book on him in two volumes, first published in 1905.

*Mühlfeld, Richard* (1856–1907), German clarinettist, in the grand-ducal orchestra at Meiningen from 1873.

*Nottebohm, Gustav* (1817–82), German musicographer. He was a friend of Mendelssohn and Schumann at Leipzig and settled in Vienna in 1846. He compiled thematic catalogues of Beethoven's and Schubert's works and wrote a book on the former's sketches.

*Pohl, Carl Ferdinand* (1819–87), German organist and musicographer. He studied in Vienna and in 1866 became librarian to the Gesellschaft der Musikfreunde there. He wrote a book on Haydn's and Mozart's visits to London and began a large biography of the former, which was finished after his death by Hugo Botstiber.

*Reinthaler, Karl Martin* (1822–96), German conductor and composer at Bremen.

*Reményi, Eduard* (1830–98), Hungarian violinist who introduced gypsy dance tunes from his country to Brahms.

*Richter, Hans* (1843–1916), Austro-Hungarian horn player and conductor, intimately associated with Wagner and later with Brahms. A frequent visitor to London and conductor of the Hallé Orchestra at Manchester in 1897–1911.

*Rietz, Julius* (1812–77), German conductor and composer. He held important conducting and teaching appointment at Düsseldorf, Leipzig and Dresden in succession.

*Scholz, Bernhard* (1835–1916), German pianist, conductor and composer. During his association with Brahms he was conductor at Breslau.

*Soldat, Marie* (born 1864), Austrian violinist. She studied with Joachim in Berlin and later settled in Vienna. She was one of the best interpreters of Brahms's violin concerto.

*Spies, Hermine* (1857–93), German mezzo-soprano singer who specialized in *Lieder*.

## Appendix C—Personalia

*Spitta, Philipp* (1841-94), German musicologist, professor of musical history at Berlin University from 1875, biographer of Bach.

*Stockhausen, Julius* (1826-1906), German baritone singer and conductor born in Paris, equally at home in German song and French opera.

*Suk, Josef* (1874-1935), Czech composer, pupil and son-in-law of Dvořák. In 1892 he formed the Bohemian Quartet, in which he played second violin.

*Tausig, Karl* (1841-71), Polish pianist, arranger and composer for his instrument.

*Treitschke, Heinrich von* (1834-96), German historian and political writer, professor at various universities, the last being Berlin.

*Widmann, Joseph Victor* (1842-1911), Swiss poet, author and critic of German descent, living at Berne.

*Wilt, Marie* (born *Liebenthaler*) (1833-91), Austrian soprano singer, first devoted to concert singing and later to opera, in which she made her début at Graz in 1865.


## APPENDIX D

### BIBLIOGRAPHY

*Antcliffe, Herbert,* 'Brahms.' (London, 1905.)
*Barth, R.,* 'Johannes Brahms und seine Musik.' (Hamburg, 1904.)
' *Briefwechsel,*' Letters, 15 vols., edited by the Brahms-Gesellschaft.
*Browne, P. A.,* 'Brahms—The Symphonies.' (Oxford, 1933.)
*Cardus, Neville,* 'Ten Composers.' (London, 1945.)
*Colles, H. C.,* 'Brahms.' (London, 1920.)
——, 'The Chamber Music of Brahms.' (Oxford, 1933.)
*Deiters, Hermann,* 'Johannes Brahms,' 2 vols. (1880). Translated and condensed into 1 vol. by Rosa Newmarch. (London, n.d.)
*Dietrich, A. and Widmann, J. V.,* 'Recollections of Johannes Brahms.' Translated by Dora Hecht. (London, 1899.)
*Ehrmann, A. von,* 'Johannes Brahms: Thematisches Verzeichnis.' (Leipzig, 1933.)
——, 'Johannes Brahms: Weg, Werk und Welt.' (Leipzig, 1933.)

*Ernest, G.,* 'Johannes Brahms.' (Berlin, 1930.)

*Evans, Edwin, sen.,* 'Handbook to the Chamber and Orchestral Music of Johannes Brahms.' (London, n.d.)

——, 'Historical, Descriptive and Analytical Account of Entire Works of Johannes Brahms,' vol. i, 'The Vocal Works.' (London, 1912.)

*Fellinger, R.,* 'Klange um Brahms.' (Berlin, 1933.)

*Friedländer, Max,* 'Brahms' Lieder.' Translated by C. Leonard Leese. (Oxford, 1929.)

——, 'Neue Volkslieder von Brahms.' (Berlin, 1926.)

*Fuller-Maitland, J. A.,* 'Johannes Brahms.' (London, 1911.)

*Geiringer, Karl,* 'Brahms: his Life and Work.' (London, 1936.)

*Gray, Cecil,* 'Johannes Brahms,' in 'The Heritage of Music,' vol. i. (Oxford, 1927 and 1948.)

*Hadow, W. H.,* 'Studies in Modern Music,' vol. ii. (London, 1926.)

——, 'Brahms and the Classical Tradition' in 'Collected Essays.' (Oxford, 1928.)

*Harrison, Julius,* 'Brahms and his Four Symphonies.' (London, 1939.)

*Henschel, George,* 'Personal Recollections of Johannes Brahms.' (Boston, 1907.)

*Hernried, R.,* 'Johannes Brahms.' (Leipzig, 1934.)

*Hill, Ralph,* 'Brahms.' (London, 1933.)

*Hirschmann, E.,* 'Johannes Brahms und die Frauen.' (Vienna, 1933.)

*Hutschenruyter, W.,* 'Johannes Brahms' (in Dutch). (The Hague, 1928.)

*Jenner, G.,* 'Johannes Brahms als Mensch, Lehrer und Künstler.' (Marburg, 1905.)

*Joachim, Joseph,* 'Letters to and from J. Joachim.' Selected and translated by Nora Bickley. (London, n.d.)

*Kalbeck, Max,* 'Brahms als Lyriker.' (Vienna, 1921.)

——, 'The Herzogenburg Correspondence,' translated by Hannah Bryant. (London, 1909.)

*Kalbeck,* 'Johannes Brahms.' 4 vols. (Berlin, 1904–14.)

*Kross, Siegfried,* 'Die Chorwerke von Johannes Brahms.' (Berlin-Halensee, 1958.)

*Landormy, Paul,* 'Brahms.' (Paris, 1921.)

*Laux, Karl,* 'Der Einsame: Johannes Brahms, Leben und Werk.' (Graz, 1944.)

*Lee, E. Markham,* 'Brahms: the Man and his Music.' (London, 1915.)

*Leyen, R. von der,* 'Johannes Brahms als Mensch und Freund.' (Düsseldorf, 1905.)

# Appendix D—Bibliography

*Litzmann, B.*, 'Clara Schumann—Johannes Brahms: Briefe aus den Jahren, 1853–96.' English translation, 'Schumann-Brahms Correspondence.' (London, n.d.)

*May, Florence,* 'The Life of Brahms,' 2 vols. (London, 1905, new ed., 1948.)

*Mies, Paul,* 'Johannes Brahms.' (Leipzig, 1930.)

——, 'Stilmomente und Ausdrucksstilformen im Brahms'schen Lied.' (Leipzig, 1923.)

*Miesner, H.,* 'Klaus Groth und die Musik: Erinnerungen an Brahms.' (Heide, 1933.)

*Miller zu Aichholz, V. von,* 'Brahms-Bilderbuch.' (Vienna, 1905.)

*Müller-Blattau, J.,* 'Johannes Brahms.' (Potsdam, 1933.)

*Murdoch, William,* 'Brahms: with an Analytical Study of the Complete Pianoforte Works.' (London, 1933.)

*Nagel, W.,* 'Die Klaviersonaten von J. Brahms.' (Stuttgart, 1915.)

——, 'Johannes Brahms.' (Stuttgart, 1928.)

*Niemann, Walter,* 'Brahms.' Translated by Catherine Alison Philips. (London, 1929.)

*Ophüls, G.,* 'Brahms-Texte.' (Berlin, 1898.)

——, 'Erinnerungen an Johannes Brahms.' (Berlin, 1921.)

*Pauli, W.,* 'Brahms.' (Berlin, 1907.)

*Perger, R. von,* 'Johannes Brahms.' (Leipzig, n.d.)

*Pulver, Jeffrey,* 'Johannes Brahms.' (London, 1933.)

*Rostand, Claude,* 'Brahms.' (Paris, 1954.)

*Schauffler, R. H.,* 'The Unknown Brahms.' (New York, 1933.)

*Schenker, Heinrich,* 'Johannes Brahms: Oktaven und Quinten.' (Vienna, 1933.)

*Schramm, W.,* 'Brahms in Detmold.' (Leipzig, 1933.)

*Smyth, Ethel,* 'Impressions that Remained.' (London, n.d.)

*Specht, Richard,* 'Brahms.' Translated by Eric Blom. (London, 1930.)

*Stephenson, K.,* 'Johannes Brahms Heimatsbekenntnis.' (Hamburg, 1933.)

*Sturke, A.,* 'Der Stil in Brahms Werken.' (Würzburg, 1932.)

*Thomas-San Galli, D. F.,* 'Johannes Brahms.' (Munich, 1922.)

*Tovey, D. F.,* 'The Chamber Music of Brahms' in Cobbett's 'Cyclopedic Survey of Chamber Music.' (Oxford, 1929.) Reprinted in Tovey's 'Essays and Lectures on Music.'

*Widmann, S. V.,* 'Johannes Brahms in Erinnerungen,' ed. by Willi Reich (Basel, 1947).

# INDEX

224

# Index

225

# Index